A Centennial History of

Rutgers
Law School
in Newark

D1206061

A CENTENNIAL HISTORY OF

RUTGERS
LAW SCHOOL
IN NEWARK

OPENING A THOUSAND DOORS

PAUL TRACTENBERG

FOREWORD BY JOHN J. FARMER JR.
DEAN, RUTGERS SCHOOL OF LAW—NEWARK

THE
History
PRESS

Published by The History Press
Charleston, SC 29403
www.historypress.net

First published 2010

Manufactured in the United States

ISBN 978.1.59629.822.4

Library of Congress Cataloging-in-Publication Data

Tractenberg, Paul L., 1938-
A centennial history of Rutgers law school in Newark : opening a thousand doors / Paul
Tractenberg.
p. cm.
Includes bibliographical references and index.
ISBN 978-1-59629-822-4
1. Rutgers Law School (Newark, N.J.)--History. 2. Law--Study and teaching--New Jersey--
Newark--History. 3. Law schools--New Jersey--Newark--History. 4. Newark (New Jersey) I.
Title.
KF292.R87T73 2010
340.071'174932--dc22
2010011657

CONTENTS

CONTENTS

FOREWORD

As a newcomer not just to the deanship of Rutgers University School of Law–Newark but to academia generally, I am possibly the least qualified of any member of the faculty or administration to write the foreword to this impressive history. I have lived through none of the triumphs and travails that have shaped this school and so can add little to the tales of colorful characters and even more colorful debates that make this book by Paul Tractenberg and his Centennial Seminar students so riveting.

I can say, however, that to read this book is to understand the special place that Rutgers Law has occupied in New Jersey's social, political and legal history. From the school's earliest days, affording a largely immigrant population the opportunity for a legal education, through its recommitment to Newark in the wake of the riots of the 1960s and its pioneering of clinical legal education and opportunity for disadvantaged students, to the present day, Rutgers School of Law–Newark has upheld three principles: opportunity, excellence and impact. This book portrays in human terms the school's commitment to those ideals and makes a persuasive case for the uniqueness of Rutgers Law's historic mission.

Professor Tractenberg's own career itself exemplifies the themes this book develops. Through his decades-long commitment to quality public education, he has helped to reshape the law in New Jersey and other states, has educated scores of law students and has had a real impact on the lives of thousands of schoolchildren. He is, in short, the perfect person to have undertaken this effort.

The fact that this book is a collaboration between a faculty member and his students also speaks volumes about the nature of the Rutgers Law experience, which at moments of crisis, transformation and triumph has involved just such collaborations for decades.

As the final chapter of the book makes clear, Rutgers School of Law–Newark enters its second century facing many challenges: how to secure its fiscal position; how to navigate a law school ratings system that either undervalues or fails entirely to consider factors that Rutgers has viewed as central to its mission; how to respond to the numerous calls for curricular reform; and how to enable its graduates to prosper in one of the most difficult job markets since the school was founded. Although it is impossible to predict how these challenges and others will be met, I am committed to meeting them with the spirit of opportunity, excellence and impact that has defined this great school throughout its history. This book is the best illustration of the adage that the past is, indeed, prologue. We will be, as we have been, electric!

John J. Farmer Jr.
April 1, 2010

Acknowledgements

T he first and foremost acknowledgment must go to the twelve law students who participated in the special Centennial Seminar I taught during academic year 2008–9. In alphabetical order, they are Heidi Alexander, Joseph Anderson, Lawrence Bellinger, Gerald Browning, Daniel Cresci (whose tragic death in March 2010 shocked and saddened all of us who knew and worked with him), Marco Franco, Steven Kroll, Shera Morgan, Tiffany Riley, Daniel Schoenberg, Dante Simone and Jonathan Stead.

This book was their idea, and their draft chapters got the ball rolling. To our delight, The History Press agreed to publish the book, and commissioning editors Kate Pluhar, Saunders Robinson and Whitney Tarella were pleasant, helpful and patient throughout a process that was longer than we expected.

Not only did my students decide that a book was feasible, but they also collaborated on two major Centennial year events—the seminar's October 20, 2008 four-hour-long program celebrating the law school's enormously important commitment to diversifying legal education and the legal profession and the afternoon session of the *Rutgers Law Review*'s April 17, 2009 symposium on innovations in legal education, focusing on Rutgers Law's equally important commitment to instilling in all of its students public interest and public service values. Heidi Alexander, a seminar member and editor in chief of the *Law Review*, played an especially important role in both programs.

Two other members of the seminar deserve special acknowledgment. Jerry Browning and Marco Franco remained active partners in the completion of this book even though they both graduated from the law school in May

2009, took their bar exams and are employed in legal jobs. This book would not have happened without their commitment and talent.

Another important partner in this enterprise has been my research assistant, Tim Kozicki, '10. For Tim, this has been a labor of love. He stepped forward to do anything and everything required.

To one of our most distinguished alumni, Elizabeth Warren, '76, we owe the book's title. In commenting on what Rutgers Law meant to her for a recent profile, she said that it "took a little kid from Oklahoma and kicked open a thousand doors for me."[1]

Many of my friends and colleagues at the law school have played important roles not only in providing information (sometimes arcane) to fill in gaps in the book but also in providing ideas and sharing reactions. Of special help have been Associate Dean and Director of the Law Library Carol Roehrenbeck; reference librarians Paul Axel-Lute and Susan Lyons; Associate Dean Fran Bouchoux; Assistant Dean Anita Walton; Manager of Public Relations Janet Donohue; alumni liaison Zahara Wadud-Pinkett; the dean's secretary, Mimi Moore; Professor and Director of Clinical Programs Jon Dubin; Professors George Thomas, Gary Francione, Frank Askin and Jonathan Hyman; and support staff members Elvirra Gallashaw and Mayra Caraballo (also my secretary). Professor Thomas deserves special kudos for reading the entire manuscript and providing some excellent suggestions.

The Law Library, in particular, has also made an enormous contribution to the school's celebration of its Centennial through its website and related activities, and I am very pleased that that website is being augmented with a section on this book. It will include a discussion board where readers and others can share their reactions to this book. Those interested can access it at http://lawwiki.rutgers.edu/100years.

Dean John Farmer graciously provided a foreword and former dean Peter Simmons submitted a long and fascinating personal reflection. Unfortunately, because of the publisher's length limitation, only Simmons's concluding paragraph could be included.

Naïvely, I entered into this project thinking that my role would be to conduct a light edit of the seminar students' submissions and to write a brief introduction and conclusion. It turned out, perhaps predictably, to involve far more intensive involvement on my part than I expected. Any errors, omissions or debatable statements, thus, are surely my responsibility.

My heavy involvement in revising student drafts and in writing far more of the text than I had planned to do meant that I have spent a good part of the past nine months on this book, including the magical month I spent during the summer of 2009 as a resident fellow at the Rockefeller Foundation's Bellagio Center overlooking Lake Como in the north of Italy. I thank and acknowledge both the Rockefeller Foundation and the amazingly supportive staff of the Bellagio Center. A copy of this book will wind up in the Bellagio Center's library bearing the blue dot signifying books written in part on-site.

Finally, I want to acknowledge the wonderful, dedicated and sometimes eccentric folks who have made one hundred years of Rutgers Law a success and delight for those of us fortunate enough to have had our professional and personal lives touched by this special place.

CHAPTER 1

THE VOICES AND VISIONS OF RUTGERS LAW SCHOOL

Rutgers School of Law–Newark reflects the history of both the city of Newark and the broader society. The school also reflects the longstanding tension in American legal education between preparing students for the practice of law and encouraging its faculty and students to think deeply, and sometimes theoretically, about the law. The pejoratives "trade school" and "university-based law school" capture the extremes of that tension.

The law school has a long history of opening its doors to working people and their children and, for more than forty years, meeting the needs of the underserved in the community and giving opportunities to those traditionally excluded from legal education and the profession. In more recent years, it has struggled to accommodate both a desire to continue to serve those "nontraditional" law students and a desire to be ranked as a top-tier school.

The challenge has been heightened by the growing financial crisis that has confronted the state of New Jersey and the nation. A relatively modest operating budget makes it ever more difficult for the law school to be a pluralistic institution effectively serving the needs of diverse students, faculty, alumni and other constituents.

This book explores the law school's triumphs and challenges throughout its one-hundred-year history. Though race, gender and socioeconomic status figure prominently in the Rutgers Law story—as does the quest for social justice—this book addresses a far wider range. The well-known work of previous chroniclers, who told the riveting stories of the "People's Electric Law School" of the '60s and '70s, figures prominently, but by then the school had been around for six decades. In its earlier years, it had faced and overcome many trying times and had experienced notable successes. Although they are less well known, many of the stories of those times are the stuff of legend. The school's founders and earlier leaders, faculty and students helped to build it up not only to survive war and economic hardship but also to thrive as it adapted to meet the challenges of civil unrest, poverty and social injustice. Throughout its history, faculty and students at Rutgers Law School have dealt with the issues of their day while continuing to engage in a program of legal education designed to expand their breadth of vision, thoughtful understanding of theory and doctrine and practical experience.

This book presents Rutgers Law's history in four chapters, each sketching out an epoch.

Chapter 2 traces the period from the school's founding as New Jersey Law School in 1908 until it was absorbed into Rutgers, the state university, in 1946 and became Rutgers School of Law–Newark ("Rutgers Law"). In the interim, there was a merger with a competitor, Mercer Beasley Law School, and the incorporation of the merged school into the University of Newark.

Chapter 3 deals with the period between 1947 and 1967, during which the school was buffeted by war and revolution: on the international level, the aftermath of World War II, the Korean War, the earlier years of the Vietnam War and, overhanging most of this period, the Cold War; and on the national, state and local levels, the riots or uprisings in many American cities, including the law school's home city of Newark.

Chapter 4 focuses on Rutgers Law's transformation between 1968 and 1977. The aftermath of the 1967 turmoil in Newark and other cities across the country led to the establishment at the school of three distinctive and continuing cornerstones—a serious commitment to a diverse student body and faculty, with an initial focus on race and socioeconomic status expanding to ethnicity and gender; the establishment of an array of law school clinical programs and other curricular innovations, including required first-year courses in Legal Representation of the Poor and International Law and Just World Order; and a growing commitment to engaging students in public interest law and in landmark federal and state cases designed to advance social justice. These augmented the school's more traditional and scholarly missions.

Chapter 5 traces Rutgers Law's evolution during the last three decades of its first one hundred years, from 1978 to 2008. The three distinctive cornerstones established in the previous decade remained prominent and, for the most part, coexisted peacefully with the school's other missions in a pluralistic environment. However, there was an assortment of challenges, even crises, that threatened the balance. Several were frontal challenges to the Minority Student Program, widely known as the MSP. But there was also the powerful and more general impact of *U.S. News & World Report*'s law school rankings since 1994 and the more recent economic tsunami of 2009–2010 that has devastated government at every level, thereby undermining support of public higher education.

Chapter 6 completes the book's treatment of the Centennial, as it begins in this introductory chapter, with the voices and visions of Rutgers Law. In Chapter 6, though, those voices speak more directly and individually, through vignette, anecdote, sadness, humor and tribute and even sometimes through recognizing individual and collective foibles. By doing so, they capture the school's heart and soul.

Chapter 7 is more forward-looking, an epilogue to the Centennial history. It takes stock of where Rutgers Law is in 2009 and then considers where the law school should go during its second one hundred years. In particular, it discusses the extent to which the law school can adapt, yet again, to new directions and new pressures while retaining the best aspects of its first one hundred years.

The voices and visions of the school, presented in this book in text and photograph, come from many sources. They include histories of the law school, the University of Newark and legal education in New Jersey; archival and other material about the school, its deans, its faculty, its students and its alumni; law school yearbooks from 1927 forward; and books, law review symposia and special events celebrating key moments in the school's history, including its Centennial year. This book also draws on an extensive literature regarding legal education in the United States and on all manner of resources regarding the social and educational context in which the law school functioned during the past one hundred years.

Much of the source material that chronicles Rutgers Law's evolution as an institution, especially beginning in the late 1960s, comes from the writings of faculty and administrators. These include autobiographies of two professors who played seminal roles in that evolution, Frank Askin and Arthur Kinoy[2]; sixteen short articles by faculty members and administrators about aspects of the "Rutgers School of Thought" that appeared in a 1999 *Rutgers Law Review* symposium anticipating the opening in 2000 of the new law building[3]; and a 2009 Centennial reminiscence in the *Rutgers Law Review* written by Professors Gary Francione and George Thomas.[4] Taken together, they reflect the diversity and pluralism of Rutgers Law and the school's continual efforts

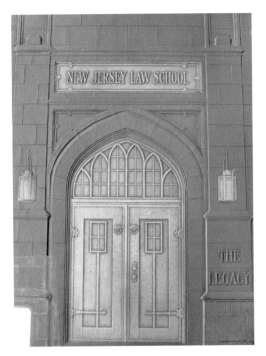

Yearbook cover from the 1930s.

to study, examine and improve both the practical and theoretical aspects of providing a high-quality legal education.

In 2008–9, Rutgers Law's Centennial year inspired a renewed effort to study the school's achievements and its influence in the legal profession and beyond. Kicking off a year of celebration, the daylong September 2008 Centennial Celebration brought together faculty members and students from years past and present, capturing the voices of the law school's history in several rounds of panel discussions and personal stories.

Professor Tractenberg's special yearlong Centennial Seminar explored the history, evolution and notable accomplishments of the law school in the broader contexts of legal education, public interest law and the press for expanded diversity in the society. The seminar, thanks to the committed efforts of the twelve enrolled students, sponsored two programs during the year, one in each semester. The first, on October 20, 2008, celebrated the law school's long and strong commitment to diversity. During a four-hour program, seventeen alumni and former faculty members, each introduced by a seminar member, spoke about the special opportunities the law school had offered them and how they took advantage of those opportunities to become leaders of bench, bar, government and politics.

The Center for Law and Justice Atrium, as viewed from the top during an event at the school. *Courtesy of Shelley Kusnetz.*

Centennial event details. *Courtesy of Shelley Kusnetz.*

In the spring semester, the Centennial Seminar assumed responsibility for the afternoon session of a daylong Centennial program sponsored by the *Rutgers Law Review* on April 17, 2009. The program's theme was the future of legal education, and in the early sessions, an array of outstanding law school deans and professors described innovative programs at their schools and prognosticated more broadly about where legal education is headed. The Centennial Seminar's afternoon session focused on the role of law schools, and especially Rutgers Law, in instilling in its students the values of public service and the use of law to advance the cause of social justice. Using an interactive, Fred Friendly–style format, with moderators challenging panelists to address provocative questions, the session brought the topic to life, fusing history with the present and future.

Speakers and crowd at a Centennial event. *Courtesy of Shelley Kusnetz.*

The videotape records of those extraordinary programs form an important part of the compilation, spearheaded by the law library, documenting and commemorating the school's Centennial. They are combined with an array of historical materials and artifacts of the school's one-hundred-year history, including archives of school newspapers, yearbooks, photographs and faculty and administrative records. A final component is a living history of the law school with interviews of current and past professors. All of these materials are available to the public on the law library's website.[5] This book aspires to be the culmination of these commemorative efforts. It seeks to recognize many of the voices and visions of Rutgers Law School over the last one hundred years and, by doing so, nourish the curiosity of future generations of law students and scholars.

CHAPTER 2

THE EARLY YEARS
(1908–1946)

*From a Start-Up Proprietary School to the
State University Law School*

When legal education began to move from the law office to the law
school, New Jersey found itself without such a school. Residents
interested in the study of law mainly crossed the river to New York City. A
young lawyer named Richard D. Currier, only a few years beyond his own
legal education in New York City, saw both a need and an entrepreneurial
opportunity for a law school in northern New Jersey. In 1908, Currier
founded the New Jersey Law School as a proprietary, or for-profit, institution.
The idea of the law school—a place of study for men and women who lived
in New Jersey and wished to enter the legal profession—was met with great
enthusiasm. Its initial emphasis on New Jersey law, practice and procedure
added to its attractiveness for residents.[6]

Initially, Currier and one of his collaborators, Percival G. Bernard, had
attempted to establish a legal education program as a division of Upsala
College. Upsala was located in Kenilworth, but the plan was to establish
the law school in Newark. According to a history of Upsala's early years,[7]
the college's board gave serious consideration to establishing a law school,
looking into the reputed characters of Currier and Bernard. Initially, a board
member reported that his own lawyer knew neither of them, but two weeks
later he reported that "they were fine characters and good researchers."[8]

Nevertheless, the effort failed because "no satisfactory arrangement could be
made with the judges who were desired as instructors."[9] Currier and Bernard
thereupon turned their attention to establishing their own freestanding law
school in Newark. At the time—the early part of the twentieth century—
Newark was New Jersey's largest city, as it is today. It had a booming economy,

Richard Currier, founder of New Jersey Law School.

a growing population and a solid infrastructure then, which made it an ideal place to launch a new law school. Thus was born New Jersey Law School. Currier served as the school's first president, and Bernard was appointed as its first dean. The school, as was common at the time, was a proprietary institution.

On October 5, 1908, thirty students began their legal education in the Prudential Building in Newark. At the time, the school had no library of its own, but the Prudential Insurance Company allowed the students access to its nine thousand volumes. However, it quickly became obvious that the facilities were inadequate for a law school, and in December of that year, the school moved to a large Victorian town house at 33 Park Street. Classes were typically scheduled for late in the day and evenings to accommodate the many students and faculty who worked full time.

In the early part of the twentieth century, American legal education and, indeed, the American legal profession were still taking shape. There were limited standards in place, or none at all. Originally, New Jersey Law School had a two-year program, and many of the students lacked not only an undergraduate degree but also any education beyond high school. Some had not even completed their high school education.

Upon completion of the two-year law program, graduates received an undergraduate Bachelor of Laws degree, LLB. The curriculum focused on the basics of law, with particular emphasis on business and commercial law.

Although New Jersey Law School was remarkable in many ways, its curriculum was not. The courses offered included many that are still staples at American law schools, such as Criminal Law, Contracts, Torts, Domestic Relations, Negotiable Instruments, Sales of Personal

Property, Real Property, Damages, Corporations, Conflict of Law, Agency, Partnership, Pleading and Practice, Bankruptcy, International Law, Evidence, Constitutional Law, Insurance, Wills and Administration and Public Service and Quasi-Public Corporations. New Jersey Law's curriculum changed very little in the early years.

In May 1909, still during the school's inaugural year, the New Jersey Board of Bar Examiners placed the institution on its list of recognized law schools, and in 1913, the New Jersey Board of Education gave the school degree-granting authority. After the first year, Percival Bernard resigned as dean and was replaced by Charles Mason.

Initially, the only requirements for admission to New Jersey Law School were that students be at least eighteen years old, have completed three years of high school and be of good moral character.

In 1913, the school's law program was extended from two to three years (or from eighteen to twenty-seven months in academic attendance). The nine additional months provided a practical advantage to budding attorneys because they were counted toward the thirty-six-month clerkship requirement to gain admission to the New Jersey Bar.

Dean Charles Mason.

JAMES A. DESMOND
Long Branch, N. J.
Prepared at Freehold (N. J.) High School.

GERALDINE DI ORIO
Newark, N. J.
Prepared at Barringer High School.

T. STAR DUNNING, JR.
Paterson, N. J.
Prepared at Paterson High School and
University School.
Delta Theta Phi Law Fraternity.

FREDA FELDMAN ROTHENBERG
Newark, N. J.
Prepared at Newark Preparatory School.

PETER M. FINE
Newark, N. J.
Prepared at Central High School.

Some 1927 graduates with lists of their high schools as preparation for New Jersey Law School.

In 1914, in response to the New Jersey Bar Association's recommendations, the law school changed its admission policy and required a high school diploma. According to an early edition of *Topics*, which was something of a school newsletter, "In 1915 there was in existence a law review, the history of which is rather obscure, evidently it went on the rocks."[10] The early academic history of the law school was apparently relatively unexceptional.

In other ways, however, it was distinctive. From the school's inception, women were admitted, although not in great numbers. The first woman graduated in 1910 with New Jersey Law's first graduating class. And it was a source of pride. In response to an article written in the *New York Times* in 1916, which asserted that none of the area law schools admitted women, the school's main founder, Richard Currier, wrote a very terse and to-the-point

Law School Lecture Hall, 1927.

letter to the editor. He stated that "our courses have been open to women ever since the school was organized."[11] Early law school publications detailing the school's history also mentioned that "[w]omen were always admitted on an equality with men." Although the causal connection is unclear, several women were named as stockholders of the proprietary school, both at its beginning and later in its history.

Just because the school admitted women, however, did not mean that it was free from period attitudes about the role of women in higher education. The 1915 mid-year examination grade report started off with the statement that the following "men" had taken it even though there were women in attendance at the time.

The first edition of *Topics* in 1925 contained the following: "Personal Notes—'Miss Harris claims the distinction of being the 'frosh mornings' only blond and although we have found that this girl from Passaic hates the fellows (?), we find that her fellow townswoman Miss Epstein is a bit more courageous."[12] That this statement appeared in a school-sanctioned student publication (in which President Currier included a call for support of the publication) speaks volumes about the place of women in the school. Still, unlike most law schools of the day, women had a place in New Jersey Law School, and as early as 1916, the school had already educated "a considerable number of women graduates successfully practicing at the New Jersey bar."[13]

In 1914, before the start of World War I, the school's student population already had increased from the thirty who began in October 1908 to about two hundred. Most came from northern New Jersey, and they were predominantly children of recent immigrants.

The school's evolution related directly to changes in the population of the city of Newark. The typical student was described as "one born in Newark, living in Newark, and likely to spend most of his days in Newark."[14]

In the early part of the twentieth century, until after World War I, Swedish, Italian and other European immigrants caused the city's population to swell. As a port city with a promising manufacturing industry, Newark was considered to have the potential to become a strong commercial center with good employment prospects.[15] This contributed to the rapid expansion of New Jersey Law, although more than half of the state's law students still attended out-of-state law schools.

Law Library, 1927.

The start of World War I caused a drastic drop in enrollment. Among the dwindling number of students in attendance, however, were some political and legal luminaries, including Aaron Lasser, who later cofounded Mercer Beasley School of Law and would become attorney general of New Jersey and mayor of Newark.

Once the war ended in 1918, New Jersey Law's enrollment quickly rebounded. In fact, by 1926–27, its student body numbered 2,335, making it the largest or second-largest law school in the United States. At that time, a competitor, Mercer Beasley Law School, was established in Newark. The establishment and eventual merger of Mercer Beasley with New Jersey Law will be described later in this chapter.

Due to the enormous enrollment increase, the law building on Park Street was torn down and replaced with a larger, Gothic structure. In addition, a new library was built on an adjoining property, and other houses in the area were purchased for classrooms and offices.

Nevertheless, even these new facilities would prove to be insufficient. In 1927, the school purchased what had been the Ballantine Brewery at 40 Rector Street. The brewery company was a longtime staple of Newark and one of the area's largest businesses before Prohibition. The brick factory building had the capacity to hold ten classrooms, two large lecture halls and a library of twenty thousand volumes.

The school had a vibrant social life in those years. The law school administration not only sought to take advantage of a spacious new building, but it also introduced morning classes and expanded school activities. There was a yearbook, a newspaper and religious organizations, as well as fraternities and sororities. Shortly thereafter, a student council was created to oversee the plethora of student activities.

In the first edition of *Topics*, a student remarked that "[i]t is considered perfectly appropriate for a green Frosh to let the world know that he is such, but we think Hendrickson is carrying it altogether too far when he carries a green pen with green ink."[16] As President Currier described it, 1925 was a year "of unusual extra-curriculum activities" at the law school.[17] The 1927 *Barrister*, a new semimonthly publication of the student council, included an advertisement for the law school's prom noting that Ozzie Nelson, who would graduate from the school in 1930 and become a well-known entertainer, would be performing at the event.[18]

On the more serious educational side, New Jersey Law decided to standardize academic ratings and reevaluate the curriculum in 1927. Due to extreme variations in essay grades, the faculty began to institute true-

The front door of the
Ballantine Brewery
Factory, a building the
law school purchased
in 1927 and occupied
between 1930 and 1947.

false, or yes-no, tests. In a 1930 report to President Currier, Dean George Harris stated that analysis backed the move to yes-no tests, which "provided mathematical norms, [and were] incapable of being affected by the caprice, bias, fatigue or varying judgment of the instructor."[19]

The school also began using standardized intelligence tests as part of the admissions process. The "Otis Self-administering Higher Examination (a highly linguistic and scholastic intelligence test), and the Inglis Vocabulary Test" were both used in the admissions process.[20] A study performed by Dean Harris showed that there was a high correlation between intelligence tests and the success of students in law school. It also showed, interestingly, that "[t]he average of the mental age of the evening division…was highest, and of the morning division was lowest."[21]

In 1928, in response to demands of the New Jersey and American Bar Associations, the law school made additional changes in its admission policy.

In addition to a high school diploma, applicants were required to have completed two years of undergraduate academic work as a prerequisite to their legal studies.

Ever the entrepreneurs, in response to these changes New Jersey Law and Richard Currier created a pre-legal department to provide potential law students with the requisite college-level education. Soon this program helped to spawn Dana College and the Seth Boyden School of Business as freestanding educational institutions.[22] In 1929, Currier opened the latter, and by 1930, Dana College was created as an undergraduate college under the control of New Jersey Law. Dana offered not only a two-year pre-legal curriculum but also a four-year program leading to a Bachelor of Arts degree, as well as a combined program in which the students could receive a BA/LLB by completing three years at Dana and one year at New Jersey Law.

Even with this impressive educational entrepreneurship, the two-year college requirement contributed to a huge enrollment decline at New Jersey Law, from the high of 2,335 students in 1926 to 878 students in 1928. Another contributing factor, no doubt, was the establishment in New Jersey of several other law schools, including the Mercer Beasley School of Law in Newark, with similar admission standards.

The Great Depression dramatically compounded the problem for New Jersey Law, as it devastated the entire country. By 1935–36, enrollment had fallen to 442. The fiscal effect was profound. For example, at its high-water mark in 1926–27, New Jersey Law's tuition revenue from freshman students alone reportedly had been more than $193,000. By 1934, tuition revenue from the entire student body was only a fraction of that amount.[23]

The seriousness of the financial situation led Currier to explore merger possibilities with other educational institutions in Newark and in New Jersey. Initially, negotiations took place with Rutgers University, not yet officially the state university. There were several reasons for Rutgers' interest in New Jersey Law, including its own lack of a law school. New Jersey Law was already well established, and its location in the state's largest city made it appealing to legislators, many of whom were New Jersey Law alumni.

However, opinion in Newark and at Dana College was decidedly negative about a merger with Rutgers. The students expressed a strong preference for an independent Newark university. There was actually a large-scale student demonstration held preceding a 1933 resolution "warning that a merger meant less academic freedom and liberalism, lower academic standards, and state regulation without commensurate state aid. In short, claimed the protesters, the college would become 'the tail end of the Rutgers kite.'"[24]

The Ballantine Brewery
and students.

A number of Dana College trustees, Essex County legislators, the state commissioner of education and the mayor of Newark shared those concerns. The mayor put it most graphically: "It looks like under the Rutgers plan we would be rather far from the base of supply. In my mind it smacks too much of the chain store system."[25]

As a result, the merger with Rutgers did not materialize at that time. Several of the main concerns voiced by merger opponents proved prophetic. The eventual merger in 1946 led to the Newark campus becoming the "tail" of the Rutgers–New Brunswick "kite," or in more current parlance, a "cash cow." And Rutgers' response to the 1950s "Red Scare," a story forthcoming in this book, clearly demonstrated that "academic freedom and liberalism" had been supplanted by conformity in the name of "patriotism."

When negotiations with other prospective institutions fell apart in the early to mid-1930s, Currier and the Dana College trustees decided to act on their own. In 1935, the trustees voted to buy out Currier and take over both New Jersey Law and the Boyden School of Business. Under the deal,

New Jersey Law retained its name, and Currier stayed on as president. Both the law school and the Boyden School of Business were converted into nonprofit institutions, which helped with the accreditation process in the future. Although some favored the name "University of Newark," the three schools would come to be known as the "Dana College Group."

MERCER BEASLEY SCHOOL OF LAW

The Mercer Beasley School of Law, named after a distinguished former chief justice of the New Jersey Supreme Court, was the creation of Aaron Lasser, Arthur T. Vanderbilt and several other prominent local attorneys, including Spaulding Frazier. They wished to start a high-quality institution that would compete with New Jersey Law. There was a perception that New Jersey Law had wandered from its educational roots and was no longer, if it ever had been, a serious educationally based institution.

Lasser, a 1918 New Jersey Law graduate, felt that his alma mater was not measuring up favorably to other area institutions. Indeed, he went so far as to call Mercer Beasley "New Jersey's first purely educational institution for the study of law."[26]

In its initial bulletin, Mercer Beasley described itself as a law school "freed from the considerations of financial returns" and one "founded upon ideals purely educational and ethical." Mercer Beasley had been incorporated as a nonprofit institution, perhaps to distinguish itself from New Jersey Law. The school's detailed mission statement underscored that it was devoted solely to educational pursuits. The tension in American legal education between the academic and professional visions thus was brought to New Jersey.

Mercer Beasley's cachet was heightened by the fact that one

Dean Spaulding Frazier.

Arthur T. Vanderbilt.

of its founders, Arthur T. Vanderbilt, a native Newarker, was a towering figure in New Jersey's legal history. He became dean of New York University Law School, was a central figure in the creation of a new state constitution in 1947 and was the first chief justice of the newly empowered New Jersey Supreme Court.

Although Mercer Beasley was committed to offering high-quality legal education, it was started on a shoestring. The incorporators obtained four rooms in the Industrial Building at 1060 Broad Street rent-free for six months. The classrooms were far from adequate, and the school was forced to move before classes even started. Mercer Beasley did not even have a library until Chief Justice William S. Gummers donated his entire personal collection of books to the school some time after its establishment.

In December 1926, Mercer Beasley's first class started with fifty students. Although the school's curriculum was almost identical to New Jersey Law's, Mercer Beasley took a markedly different approach to legal education. "The mere accumulation of information is subordinated to the more important end of developing the faculties of the student, and of training him in habits of legal reasoning."[27]

The method of instruction surely was inventive. Every course used a combination of lecture and case method, with two instructors co-teaching—one using the lecture method for half of the period and the other teaching the case method for the other half. Interestingly, the faculty members were all graduates of (the supposedly inadequate) New Jersey Law.

Despite Mercer Beasley's small enrollment, it became a successful law school and featured a surprisingly large array of student activities, including a yearbook, a law review, a student council and even a basketball team. It also had organizations relating to legal practice, including moot court, rather than socially oriented fraternities and sororities. Unlike New Jersey Law, Mercer Beasley's student population did not decline during the Depression.

Almost from its founding, the trustees of Mercer Beasley sought to combine with a larger institution to ensure the school's financial stability. In September 1933, it accomplished its mission when Mercer Beasley merged with the Newark Institute of Arts and Science. By July of the following year, the two schools officially formed the University of Newark, and Mercer Beasley moved to Newark Institute's home in the Academy Building, 17–25 Academy Street.

This new alignment of higher education institutions in Newark set the stage for a grand merger of the Dana College Group and the University of Newark in 1936.

THE UNIVERSITY OF NEWARK MERGES WITH THE DANA COLLEGE GROUP

As early as the spring of 1934, students and faculty at the Dana College Group and at the University of Newark, as well as prominent local citizens, had begun demanding that these schools form a single university. Shortly thereafter, negotiations began, but by that summer they had stalled, apparently because Currier demanded to be made president of the merged institution for ten years, which was unacceptable to the University of Newark. Later that year, the Dana College Group Board of Trustees paved the way to a merger by replacing Currier with Dr. Frank Kingdon.

By 1936, all of the financial and practical arrangements had been completed, and the five entities composing the two groups of colleges became one University of Newark with three new divisions: the College of Arts and Sciences, the Law School and the School of Business. The law school was a combination of Mercer Beasley and New Jersey Law School, each of which had its own dean.

The merger had its frictions and conflicts, however, especially resulting from the anger and disappointment of those who had been administrators, faculty and students at New Jersey Law. The March 18, 1936 issue of the *Barrister* contained two letters, a long article and an editorial documenting them. One letter was from Richard Currier resigning from the University of Newark's board of trustees and decrying both "the rape of New Jersey Law School" and the ouster of its dean, George Harris, in favor of Mercer

Dean George Harris.

Beasley's Spaulding Frazier. The second letter was from President Frank Kingdon and sought to calm the roiled waters by indicating that key decisions were yet to be made about the operation of the new merged law school. The article and editorial recounted the students' perceptions of the elements of the crisis and their strong concerns.

Apparently, the two-dean problem was resolved by a decision that the deanship would go first to New Jersey Law's Harris and then to Mercer Beasley's Frazier. The newly merged University of Newark School of Law was located at 40 Rector Street. It benefited from the joining of faculties and resources, immediately creating a much stronger institution, and the merged law school was able to provide a greater range of advanced courses beginning in 1937.

STRUGGLES FOR THE SCHOOL OF LAW

Despite some immediate and obvious benefits of merger, the unified law school's initial success was quickly undermined by hard times. This was typical of Rutgers Law's one-hundred-year history—periods of great success alternated with periods of great challenges.

The academic year of 1938–39 saw the start of an enrollment decline that persisted every year until the end of World War II. On the eve of the war, total enrollment dipped below two hundred students. In 1930, New Jersey Law itself had graduated more students.[28]

Furthermore, because the law school was so intertwined with the other institutions of the University of Newark, its accreditation was delayed. The

American Bar Association (ABA), as accrediting agency, gave three reasons for its initial refusal to accredit the merged law school: failure of the other University of Newark colleges to receive Middle States accreditation, the law school's lack of a separate law library and the financial difficulties plaguing the University of Newark as a whole.

During the summer of 1939 and thereafter, the law school continued pursuing its goal of acquiring ABA accreditation. On the library front, it dramatically increased the law collection and, through extensive renovations, provided additional space for library stacks and study areas. To alleviate financial difficulties, the law school sought to increase tuition revenue by establishing a four-year evening program. Several times in years since then, that program has become a hot-button issue.

Finally, in December 1941, after the other colleges of the University of Newark received Middle States approval, the law school was granted accreditation by the ABA; later in that same month, it was approved for membership in the Association of American Law Schools (AALS).

Despite receiving accreditation, law school enrollment continued to decline during the war years. At its lowest point, during the 1943–44 academic year, the school had only thirty-seven students, and it graduated eight, thirteen and fourteen students in 1944, 1945 and 1946, respectively. A year before the end of the war, there was concern about the school's financing and possible loss of accreditation due to an inability to meet minimum faculty requirements. In response, the trustees made three suggestions about how to decrease expenses and increase income: dispense with a full-time librarian and have faculty operate the library; have full-time faculty provide all instruction; and eliminate community extension courses.

THE UNIVERSITY OF NEWARK MERGES WITH RUTGERS UNIVERSITY

The end of World War II improved the financial state and overall landscape of the University of Newark School of Law. The school paid off its mortgage and was now awaiting an influx of new applicants, mostly returning veterans. Although accredited and debt-free, the law school needed help to handle the influx of new students. Due in large part to the state legislators' desire for unification of New Jersey's higher educational resources, Rutgers (the newly minted state university) began anew to explore the possibility of a merger with the University of Newark. This would provide Rutgers with the state's

A Victorian mansion, formerly owned by the Ballantine Brewery Company, which the law school occupied between 1947 and 1956.

only fully accredited law school at the time. This time around, the University of Newark was very receptive to a merger, especially after the financial troubles through which it had struggled. It saw affiliation with a major state university as a way to ensure financial stability and increase prestige.

On July 1, 1946, the University of Newark became a part of Rutgers University. Shortly thereafter, it was decided that the law school would function best, and have a more secure identity, if it were separated from the other Newark units. As a consequence, Rutgers Law moved to a three-story Victorian mansion on 37 Washington Street.

Enrollment, however, continued to grow, primarily because of the influx of veterans. For example, in 1946, out of a total of 391 students, 311, or almost 80 percent, were veterans. Of the 80 nonveterans, 10 were women.[29] By 1956, the school had outgrown its facilities, and it moved again, this time to what had been a YWCA at 53 Washington Street. Thus, the law school's history of outgrowing new buildings continued (although it seemed to alternate with sharp enrollment declines).

CHAPTER 3

THE TUMULTUOUS MIDDLE YEARS (1947–1967)

*Rutgers Law Contends with Postwar Booms,
Hot and Cold Wars and Urban Upheaval*

This period was bookended by a world war on one side and urban upheavals on the other. In between, the law school had to contend with the effects of a variety of hot and cold wars: the Cold War proper, which many date from the end of World War II to as late as 1991, with the period between 1953 and 1962 sometimes referred to as the period of crisis and escalation; the Korean War between 1950 and 1953; and the Vietnam War, with U.S. military advisers being sent there as early as 1950, U.S. involvement escalating in the early 1960s and U.S. combat units being deployed in 1965.

The post–World War II enrollment level at Rutgers Law was maintained throughout the next decade as the school grew into its new role and status as the state university law school.

In 1951, Alfred C. Clapp—a prominent lawyer, state senator and professor of law intermittently at Mercer Beasley and Rutgers Law from 1929 until 1971—became dean of the law school, until his appointment just two years later to the Appellate Division of the New Jersey Superior Court. Clapp provided the law school with high visibility leadership. He was a recognized leader of the bar, presiding over the Essex County Bar Association and serving as editor of the *New Jersey Law Journal* at the time of his appointment to the deanship. Periodically, he was pressed into service to assist with state constitutional modifications as both counsel to the legislature in 1944 and as a convention delegate in 1947 and 1966. Clapp also was very active in state Republican political circles, serving as legal counsel or campaign manager for a number of candidates for office, including Governor Thomas Kean.

A 1949 yearbook photo.

In 1953, Lehan K. Tunks, a more traditional legal academic and the holder of a doctorate in judicial science from Yale, became dean. He served until 1962, supervising the school's steady growth and emphasizing an academic approach to the study of law (although he did recognize the need to prepare students for law practice).

Rutgers School of Law—Camden

During the 1950s, an interesting dimension was added to Rutgers Law: a south Jersey division. The South Jersey School of Law had been established in 1926, the same year as Mercer Beasley. South Jersey Law primarily served an area in the southern part of the state and in Bucks County, Pennsylvania. For more than twenty years, it had a fluctuating enrollment of about one hundred students.

In 1950, four years after the incorporation of the University of Newark into Rutgers University, the South Jersey School of Law itself became part of the Rutgers family. It was merged with the law school in Newark, and the dean in Newark led both "campuses." Professors moved back and forth between them, and the dean regularly attended staff meetings held by the South Jersey Division (as it was then known). Even "[t]he Association of American Law Schools consider[ed] the two divisions of the Rutgers University School of Law to be a single school" in its 1960 accreditation report.[30]

In the mid-1950s, average attendance at the South Jersey Division plummeted to about forty students, and Dean Tunks was prompted to make several recommendations for dealing with the situation. One was to incorporate the South Jersey Division into the Newark Division (which he acknowledged was little different from closing it down). Another was to infuse the South Jersey Division with more money to help it grow into a more stable institution. In his 1958 report, Tunks projected that the South Jersey Division would lose about $300,000 over the next three years.[31] The response by Rutgers was to attempt to close the school. The plan was "to admit no freshman to the school next fall [of 1959] and to close the school entirely after graduation of the class of 1961."[32] Those plans were scuttled, however, when Rutgers president Mason Gross failed to convince the legislative appropriations committee that the South Jersey Division should be closed. Instead, the committee voted to "use phraseology in its 1959–60 budget bill which it [felt would] stymie Rutgers University's proposed shut down of the South Jersey Law School in Camden."[33]

The school stayed open and was slowly nursed back to health. The 1960 and 1961 books were balanced by "state or municipal appropriations" totaling almost $100,000 per year. Starting in 1961, the school began to grow quite rapidly until it rivaled enrollment in Newark. In 1967, Russell Fairbanks was appointed as dean of Rutgers School of Law–Camden, and by action of the Rutgers Board of Governors, Rutgers–Camden Law became an autonomous school, with independent accreditation and its own law journal. Ever since, the schools have been separate institutions with surprisingly little contact. Rutgers Law in Newark tends to gravitate toward the law schools of New York City and Rutgers Law in Camden toward Philadelphia. The two schools today share nothing of the close relationship they once had.

ASPIRING TO BE A "UNIVERSITY LAW SCHOOL"

During the decade starting in the mid-1950s, drastic changes, or their possibility, were not limited to the Camden campus, however. In Newark, there were serious discussions about both closing down the night school program and moving the school to New Brunswick, the main Rutgers campus. Both reflected a desire on the part of Dean Tunks and some members of the law faculty to achieve higher status as a "university law school."

Tunks acknowledged in a 1955 letter to the law school trustees that one of his initial goals upon being appointed in 1953 was to end the night school program. He proposed the "quiet cessation of accepting" applicants to the program, which is exactly what happened. A letter from him to several faculty members illustrates how important this accomplishment was to his vision of the school. While talking about the night school, he said, "I believe that we are pretty sure (cross your fingers) to be able to get rid of it, but the question is when."[34]

In a memorandum about the night school program, Tunks explained why he was determined to eliminate it: "A night law school provides sub-standard legal education inappropriate to the high objectives of a university."[35] The specter of tired professors inadequately teaching tired and inadequately prepared students overhung the discussion. Tunks also said that the night school "consume[d] precious resources" and stood in the way of developing a great full-time university law school.[36]

That made manifest the tension between "university law schools" and those disparaged by some as merely "trade schools"; in Dean Tunks, Rutgers

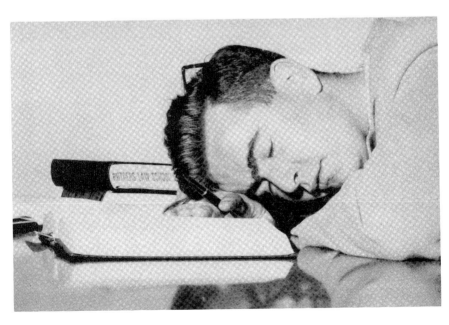

Student sleeping, 1951 yearbook.

Student studying, 1951
yearbook.

Law had an avowed champion of the university law school. One can only guess how he would react today to the law school's vibrant and highly regarded night school, or part-time, program.

Just as Tunks and others at Rutgers Law spoke out strongly against the night school program, there were those against keeping the law school in Newark. Tunks predicted that the school could not survive unless it was moved to New Brunswick. There was a feeling that the Newark–New York City area had many metropolitan schools and very few campus-based schools. Some thought that the law school was more likely to attract serious, academically motivated students if it were relocated to New Brunswick. A city campus was thought to attract those more interested in partying than in studying law.

In a 1954 report, the law school's Committee on Building Plans and the dean recommended that the school move to a new building in New Brunswick. In 1958, the law school's Committee on Planning and Development repeated the recommendation. Its reasons included that the school would attract higher-quality students because of the availability of residential facilities; the increased programming flexibility and financial support; and the ability to recruit higher-quality staff.[37]

The move to New Brunswick never materialized, though. Various explanations were proffered: New Brunswick was close enough to Camden to threaten the legal program there, and Newark, the state's largest city, should have its own law school. Ultimately, the state's political alignments might have been the justification, as they explained the survival of a struggling South Jersey Law School. Whatever the reason, Rutgers Law remains in

Newark, where it and its predecessor schools have been for one hundred years—and this is true despite occasional resurrections of the idea of a move to New Brunswick, perhaps as a consolidated Rutgers Law School, or even to Princeton.

During the Cold War

The period between the merger of the University of Newark with Rutgers and the Newark Riots of 1967 proved to be one of great contrasts for the law school. For the first time, the *Rutgers Law Review* named in 1951 an evening student as its editor in chief, the most prestigious student honor. Yet, only a few years later, in 1955, Rutgers Law eliminated the evening program, and it took a legislative mandate to reestablish it in 1975. Paradoxically, Rutgers Law has been named recently one of the nation's most welcoming schools for part-time students.

The most significant contrast during this period, however, is the one between the school's early capitulation to attacks on the academic freedom (and first amendment rights) of its faculty during the Red Scare and the role its faculty played in fighting such attacks in later years. This is most memorably captured in a photo of Rutgers professor Arthur Kinoy's forcible removal from the House Un-American Activities Committee (HUAC) in 1966. Professor Kinoy traveled to the capitol to defend Linus Pauling at the HUAC hearings. He and other Rutgers Law professors were instrumental in Pauling's vindication in the face of charges that he was involved with Communist groups.[38] Their work would lay a foundation for the coming decades of activism back in New Jersey. The work of Kinoy and others at the law school gave it a reputation as a leader in the defense of constitutional rights. The school's earlier leadership role in embracing Red Scare assaults on civil rights, however, is neither as well known nor as commendable.

The beginning of this ignoble period in the law school's history began elsewhere on the Rutgers–Newark campus.[39] In 1951, M.I. Finley, an assistant professor of history, was accused by two former Communist academics of having led a Communist study group while he was a graduate student at Columbia during the 1930s and of having organized "some communist front organizations." Finley explained to Rutgers administrators the real nature of these groups, and when he was subpoenaed to appear before the McCarran Committee (a U.S. Senate counterpart to HUAC), he was assured by a Rutgers dean "not to worry." In his appearance before the committee, Finley testified that he was not then a Communist but refused to say whether he had ever been one and refused to name anyone else. His testimony attracted little attention at the time. Six months later, in 1952, Simon Heimlich, an associate professor of physics and mathematics at Rutgers–Newark, was also called to testify before the McCarran Committee. He suspected that it was because someone at Rutgers had a personal vendetta against him. Later information suggested that there may have been a Federal Bureau of Investigation (FBI) informant at Rutgers. Although Heimlich informed Rutgers president Lewis Webster Jones that he was not then nor had ever been a Communist, he refused, on principle, to answer

Professor Arthur Kinoy.

any questions when he appeared before the committee, invoking his Fifth Amendment right against self-incrimination.

There was an outcry at Rutgers over Heimlich's refusal, which focused attention back on Finley as well. As a consequence, President Jones set in motion a review process. Within two weeks, a special faculty review committee concluded that "no charges should be preferred" and that "no further action should be taken."

The Rutgers Board of Trustees had a different view, however. Responding to great political and public pressure—and to the admonition of the university's counsel that Rutgers "cannot offend public opinion"—the trustees adopted a resolution making it grounds for immediate dismissal if any member of the faculty or staff refused "on the ground of the Fifth Amendment…to answer any questions propounded by any duly constituted investigatory body relating to whether he is, or has been, a member of the Communist Party." The resolution further stated that "there is no place on the faculty of Rutgers University for a member of the Communist Party, or for anyone who is under its discipline."

The trustees gave Finley and Heimlich nineteen days within which they had to agree to testify or be fired. When they declined to testify, they were fired. Although that ended Heimlich's academic career, Finley went on to a distinguished career at Cambridge University, and in 1979, he was knighted.

The Red Scare reached the law school in 1953 when Associate Professor Abraham Glasser was called to testify before HUAC. Glasser had previously been accused of being a Communist spy when he was an attorney at the Department of Justice in 1938 and 1939, and he was exonerated of the charges. Glasser stood on principle and refused to tell HUAC more than that he was not at that time "an actual card-carrying, official member of the Communist party." He refused to answer further questions on numerous grounds, including the Fifth Amendment. According to the *New York Times*, "The Professor's tactics evoked the displeasure of his questioners and the smiles of the committee members soon began to look forced." The *Times* also wrote that "Professor Glasser puffed his pipe and seemed to enjoy the situation, but no more than did his counsel, Leonard B. Boudin of New York. Amid incessant clashes, the 37-year-old professor was accused of giving argument and debate where one-word responses would have sufficed for the record."

On March 19, 1953, the day after Glasser's HUAC testimony, he was suspended by Rutgers president Jones. On April 30, Jones announced formal charges against Glasser, which were referred to a law school faculty committee. The committee's mandate was to make recommendations to the board of trustees about: (1) whether Glasser had violated the board's resolution regarding refusal to testify, and (2) whether there were extenuating circumstances that would justify not applying the board's resolution. The committee answered the questions narrowly, finding that Glasser had violated the resolution and that there were no special circumstances exempting Glasser from it. The committee did, however, note that unusual circumstances were present, including Glasser's previous exoneration and the bias and harassment to which Glasser was subjected by Congressional investigators. The committee recommended that Glasser be allowed to resign, which he did.

Rutgers' treatment of Finley, Heimlich and Glasser drew praise from HUAC but condemnation from the American Association of University

Professors (AAUP), which censured Rutgers in 1956. Later that year, Rutgers was reorganized, and its board of trustees was largely replaced by a board of governors. A special committee of the new board, headed by a former Superior Court judge, issued a report to the Association of American Law Schools, acknowledging that the school's treatment of Glasser "had not met association standards" but denying that his resignation in response to the threat of termination was "coerced." The AALS formally censured Rutgers in 1958, accepting the first of the report's contentions but not the second. The association found that it was "a violation of academic due process to put a faculty member to such a choice."

Prior to the AALS censure, Rutgers' new board of governors reversed the resolution of the old board of trustees, which had been the basis for Glasser's firing, and Glasser thereafter requested a rehearing. His request was supported by a unanimous vote of the law school's faculty and by the AALS, but the board rejected it. Glasser had hoped that the then pending censure by the AALS would sway what the *Times* called "two or three 'adamant' individuals at Rutgers to a rehearing." Tragically, according to Glasser's wife at the time, writer Judith Viorst (educated at Rutgers–Newark), the board's refusal to reopen the matter destroyed Glasser's career.

The work of Arthur Kinoy and other Rutgers Law faculty in the mid-1960s in resisting the Red Scare and HUAC at least partly offset this sorry chapter in Rutgers' history. This progressive effort to recognize and enforce constitutional rights took other forms as well in those years.

The school donated office space to the newly constituted Newark Legal Services Project (NLSP) in 1966, after having been involved in the project's formation in 1965. In support of its primary work of providing legal representation to the poor of Newark, NLSP established a program in 1966 that allowed third-year law students to participate in small claims court matters under the guidance of NLSP attorneys.[40] Even before then, though—beginning in the late 1950s—the law school had an indigent defendant program under which twenty-eight students assisted in representing indigents in court.[41]

Rutgers Law's developing reputation for progressivism during the early 1960s reached as far as Robert Kennedy, then the United States attorney general. In 1961, soon after he assumed his position, Kennedy became concerned about the lack of black lawyers in the Department of Justice. He wrote to Dean Tunks at Rutgers Law stating that, although he did not want to employ anyone simply because of their race, he did want to break down barriers in the Justice Department. Tunks replied by providing names

The Young
Women's Christian
Association
building, which
was home to the
law school between
1956 and 1965.

of four graduates who might be interested in positions there, all of whom "happen[ed] to be black."[42]

This is not to suggest that in the early to mid-1960s the law school had become an extremely liberal institution. Rather, it was a school just beginning a transition, a transition that accelerated with a vengeance starting in 1967 with the urban upheavals that shattered Newark and other cities in New Jersey and throughout the country. Until then, there were regular reminders that Rutgers Law was a quite traditional, predominantly white school that had begun to elevate its aspiration to be a higher-status university law school above its commitment to enforcing constitutional rights, representing the poor and working for social justice.

Illustratively, in 1967, near the height of the Vietnam War, the school barred the teaching of a seminar on "draft dodging." Also, the departures of faculty members for prestigious positions with other, more elite, law schools and with government agencies were seen as a sign of status and progress. So the departures in 1962 of both Professor Allan Axelrod for Yale Law School (temporarily) and of Professor Clarence Clyde Ferguson, Rutgers Law's first black faculty member, to become general counsel of the United States Commission on Civil Rights were viewed more as pluses than minuses. Rutgers Law was Axelrod's home base, however, for most of his law teaching career until his recent death. Ferguson went on to a renowned career in law and public affairs as dean of Howard Law School, a Harvard Law School distinguished professor and U.S. ambassador to Uganda, among other major positions.

The possibility that another prominent member of the faculty, Professor Robert Knowlton, might leave produced an interesting turnabout. Apparently, Knowlton had been offered a position at New York University Law School with a significant salary increase. Knowlton rejected the NYU offer, however, prompting Dean Tunks to state in a letter to the president of Rutgers that Knowlton had remained at Rutgers Law, at least in part, because it no longer had an evening school, whereas NYU did. According to Tunks, a champion of eliminating the evening school, this reflected Knowlton's "aversion to night law school plants."[43]

By the 1964–65 school year, the law school had two distinguished tenured women (Ruth Bader Ginsburg and Eva H. Morreale) on a faculty of about twenty-five, a better percentage than most law schools at the time. This foreshadowed a commitment to a faculty diverse in gender and racial terms. Professor Ginsburg (now U.S. Supreme Court justice) was on the Rutgers Law faculty for nine years and was instrumental in developing the school's— and her own—engagement with gender equality issues. Professor Morreale, now Hanks, also taught at Rutgers Law for an extended period until 1976, when she moved to Cardozo School of Law, where she continues to be a member of the faculty.

Other faculty luminaries of this period (in alphabetical order) included Alfred Blumrosen, Alexander Brooks, Victor Brudney, Marvin Chirelstein, Julius Cohen, Thomas Cowan, David Haber, Eli Jarmel, Robert Knowlton, Saul Mendlovitz, Gerald Moran, Sidney Posel and J. Allen Smith. They were an intellectually and professionally diverse group, but they were white males all.

The students, too, during the 1950s and early 1960s were primarily white and male, with a consistent but relatively small smattering of women and blacks. More than many law schools, though, they tended to retain a working-class character. The end of the night law program changed that a bit, but not completely. The other overwhelming characteristic was that the student body was local—a commuter group—since there were no dormitories.

Professor Ruth Bader Ginsburg.

For a long time, the law school's population largely mirrored Newark's, even as the characteristics of Newarkers were in constant flux over the law school's first sixty years. That began to change, however, by the mid-1960s, and the change accelerated dramatically by the late 1960s. By way of example, during those sixty years and beyond, Newark evolved from a European immigrant enclave to a city that, at the 2000 census, was 53 percent African American.[44] Rutgers Law had to scurry to try to continue its tradition of mirroring Newark's population.

In the mid-1960s, at about the same time as Professor Kinoy's constitutional battles in Washington began in earnest, the first large waves of African Americans began to arrive in Newark from the South.[45] It was challenging for the newcomers to establish businesses and other economic enterprises since many existing residents viewed them as threatening and "different." The Italian-American community, especially in the North Ward, and the Eastern European and then Spanish and Portuguese communities of the East Ward, held firm; most of the new arrivals gravitated to the Central and South Wards.

In the South Ward, during the late 1960s and early 1970s, the new Newarkers from the South replaced the dominant Jewish population. The effect was that Newark increasingly became divided along racial and, to a considerable extent, social class lines. The seeds were planted for the events of 1967 and 1968, and Rutgers Law—and the Rutgers–Newark campus of which it was a part—was at the center of the fray, geographically and otherwise.

Upheaval, Trauma and the Beginnings of Change

Rutgers, incidentally, was not an innocent bystander to these developments. Thousands of residents in the area of the Newark campus lost their homes as Rutgers–Newark expanded through the use of the state's eminent domain power, and a new Rutgers Law building, dedicated in September 1966, was a significant part of the Rutgers expansion. Combined with the growing disparities between the racial and social class composition of the remaining neighborhoods and the school, this led to heightened tension. After all, sitting in the midst of dwindling and deteriorating residential areas for relatively low-income African American residents was a nearly all-white institution whose predominant mission was a traditional one: to prepare white lawyers to serve white clients mainly in commercial matters.

Although a seminar on civil rights was offered at Rutgers Law as early as 1958, and the mid-1960s, as described previously, encouraged some faculty and student involvement in representing indigent defendants and in protecting other constitutional rights, this could not alter the perception that the school offered little to its neighboring communities in services or access to educational opportunities.

Even Rutgers Law's then new building was described by some as fortresslike, designed to keep out the surrounding minority community. This fifty-thousand-square-foot structure was the first building built expressly for the law school since the early years of New Jersey Law. Named Ackerson Hall after New Jersey Supreme Court justice Henry E. Ackerson, who arranged for much of the funding, it provided ample room for the student population of about 350. Within a decade, however, the building became unmanageably overcrowded as the school's enrollment almost doubled and the law library's collection grew apace. And so the school's days as a vagabond continued.

In 1979, the law school once again relocated to a building constructed for other purposes—the seventeen-story Firemen's Fund Insurance Company

Ackerson Hall, which housed the law school between 1965 and 1979.

high-rise. Although it had a certain charm that appealed to some, it never quite worked as a law school, and its elevators rarely worked at all. Yet, it was twenty years before Rutgers Law moved to its current building, undoubtedly the best-suited for a law school in its one-hundred-year history. But that's getting ahead of the story.

In the summer of 1967, tensions reached the boiling point in Newark. Of course, Rutgers Law and the Rutgers–Newark campus were, in a sense, bit players in a large-scale drama, but that doesn't mean they didn't contribute to it or become engaged in it.

Violence erupted one hot evening after a black cab driver, John Smith, was arrested for tailgating a police car, and a rumor spread rapidly that he had been beaten to death by police. He had, in fact, been transported to a local hospital. Regardless, the news and rumors brought simmering tensions to a breaking point and resulted in five days of violence, looting and chaos. The riots left twenty-six people dead and hundreds injured.[46]

The riots defined the 1960s in Newark.[47] They brought to light the misery of poverty, the city's public housing crisis, the substandard public education, the inadequate healthcare and the ubiquitous unemployment that shaped most black Newarkers' lives.

Even after the acute tensions had ceased, the city's residents dealt with the results in their own way. Black residents grappled with the devolution of their community, now in disarray. "White flight" began in earnest, as the families of European immigrants, who had lived and worked in Newark in previous generations, escaped to the nearby suburbs. Just weeks after the riots, a business owner was quoted in the *New York Times* as predicting "[a]t least 50 per cent of these people [with businesses] will close up completely or move to the suburbs."[48] His prediction probably understated the reality that emerged.

As the racial balance of Newark shifted, so did the city's political guard. Hugh Addonizio was voted out of the mayor's office, leaving behind a legacy

Dean Willard Heckel.

of corruption in city hall. He would be the last nonblack mayor of Newark (at least to the present time).[49]

At the same time, administrators, professors and students at Rutgers Law, who were still predominantly white and male, stepped forward, in many cases for the first time, to engage themselves in the problems of an unraveling city. They worked with community and activist groups to bring their legal and human skills to bear on the problems of Newark residents caught up in the aftermath of the July 1967 upheavals.

The law school's dean, Willard Heckel, led the effort at Rutgers Law and, in short order, wound up as the head of Newark's federal anti-poverty agency, the United Community Corporation.[50] Heckel's efforts were combined with those of his longtime partner, Malcolm Talbott, who had served as a university vice-president in charge of the Rutgers–Newark campus beginning in 1963 after a long career as a Rutgers Law professor.[51] Shortly after the 1967 riots, Talbott became co-chair of the Committee of Concern with Oliver Lofton, a black attorney serving as administrative director of the Newark Legal Services Project. Formed by sixty community leaders, who elected the co-chairs, the committee quickly grew to six hundred members from all walks of life. New Jersey's governor, Richard Hughes, himself a 1931 graduate of the law school, authorized the committee to investigate the causes of the riots and recommend possible social and economic improvements.

The extraordinary involvement and commitment of Heckel and Talbott, when added to the earlier national work of Arthur Kinoy, inspired increasing activism by Rutgers Law's faculty and students and paved the way for a transformation of the school.

CHAPTER 4

THE YEARS OF TRANSFORMATION (1968–1977)

From a Traditional White Male Commuter School to the "People's Electric Law School"

The 1967 Newark riots and their aftermath triggered multifaceted and far-reaching changes at Rutgers–Newark and Rutgers Law. Two linked events symbolized the transformation particularly dramatically—the protests and ultimate takeover of Conklin Hall by the undergraduate Black Organization of Students (BOS) between the spring of 1968 and the spring of 1969 and the indictment of the law school by the Association of Black Law Students (ABLS) in early November 1969 that precipitated extraordinary introspection, debate and fundamental changes at Rutgers Law   That these student protests had the effect they did is all the more remarkable because there were so few black students on campus, and they were so recently arrived. As late as 1967, of 2,500 undergraduate students at Rutgers–Newark, only 62 were black; just a few years earlier there were only 20. There were also no black faculty members. The situation at the law school was only slightly better regarding students and no better regarding faculty.

At the same time, though, the external world was experiencing cataclysmic changes, even beyond the urban upheavals, that had a powerful impact on all Americans. On April 4, 1968, Dr. Martin Luther King Jr. was assassinated. Only two months later, on June 6, 1968, Robert F. Kennedy met a similar fate. On a broader scale, the Vietnam War was continuing to escalate and provoke widespread protests by students, young people and many others of all ages and colors.

The story of the undergraduate protests at Rutgers–Newark and their great impact is an important one. It is well documented by the eminent historian Professor Richard P. McCormick in his book *The Black Student Protest*

Movement at Rutgers.[52] McCormick was the father of current Rutgers president Richard L. McCormick. As to Rutgers–Newark in particular, the scope and impact of the BOS protest is best dramatized by a March 3, 1969 press release issued by Vice-President Talbott detailing the university's favorable response to ten of BOS's twelve demands.[53]

The focus of this book, however, is on Rutgers Law, and that is the main thrust of this chapter. Even before ABLS issued its formal "Indictment," the law school had begun to broaden and modernize its programs of study and make other changes in response to the Newark riots and resulting student demands. In 1968, the curriculum was expanded to include courses and seminars such as Legal Representation of the Poor, Social Legislation, Urban Poverty, Consumer Credit and the Poor, Law and Psychoanalytic Theory and Work of the Juvenile Court. In 1969, first-year students were required to enroll in either Legal Representation of the Poor, Legal Process or Legal Writing. Upper-level course offerings included courses on welfare law administration and rehabilitation techniques in juvenile courts and seminars on civil liberties and constitutional litigation.

As some of these courses and seminars suggest, the law school was broadening its social change efforts beyond the classroom and beginning to engage students in the real world of public interest advocacy through the courts, administrative agencies and legislative bodies, an approach that soon became a hallmark of Rutgers Law.

One of the early connections was with the Welfare Rights Project. Another had a regional perspective through PENJERDEL, an organization serving parts of Pennsylvania, New Jersey and Delaware. Reaching much farther afield was the World Order Models Project (WOMP), a program directed by Rutgers Law professor Saul Mendlovitz. In 1968, WOMP had its first meeting in New Delhi, India. The program was created to develop models "in which war has been eliminated as an acceptable social institution and in which tolerable conditions of worldwide economic and social justice have been achieved."[54]

THE MINORITY STUDENT PROGRAM

The year 1968 also marked the beginning of a serious and long-overdue effort to racially diversify the law school and the legal profession. The need was obvious and profound. Between 1960 and 1967, only twelve nonwhite students graduated from Rutgers Law. Given that the law school was a major preparer of New Jersey lawyers, it was hardly surprising that, as of 1969, there were fewer than sixty African American attorneys among the eight thousand practicing in the state and even fewer Hispanic and Asian-American attorneys.

Rutgers Law took on the challenge directly. It recognized that the problem was systemic. "Facing squarely the fact that the reliance by law schools on traditional admissions criteria had had the effect of nearly excluding members of minority groups from legal education," the law school faculty created the Minority Student Program (MSP).[55] The MSP was one of the first of its kind in the country, making Rutgers Law a nationally recognized leader in providing legal education for minorities and the disadvantaged.

While most other law schools just increased their recruitment efforts to search for minority applicants who met traditional admissions standards, Rutgers Law broadened its admissions standards to include a far greater span of society. The creators of the MSP recognized that reducing reliance on traditional standards—primarily the Law School Aptitude Test (LSAT) score and Undergraduate Grade Point Average (UGPA)—was the only viable means of substantially enlarging the pool of those likely to be admitted to law school.

The MSP was created to admit students on an experimental basis, using broadened criteria. The LSAT and UGPA were still part of the mix, but increased weight was given to other factors, such as leadership potential, business and professional experience, age, involvement in community affairs and personal recommendations. The MSP's initial focus was disadvantaged African American applicants, but over the years, Hispanic-Americans, Asian-Americans and Native Americans were included. Eventually, factors other than race or ethnic background were also considered, such as coming from low-income families or having been educationally disadvantaged.

The MSP began in the fall of 1968. In a letter to Dean Russell Fairbanks of the newly autonomous Rutgers–Camden Law School, Dean Heckel reported that the Newark law faculty had voted to implement a plan for admitting black students starting that fall. The plan was to reserve 20 seats for black students of a total of 150 in the entering class.[56] Actually, that September, 23 black students were admitted under the special program standards. Two months later, in November 1968, the school committed itself to a five-year "plan to double the number of negro and minority group attorneys in the state of New Jersey. The plan [would] cost $498,400, mainly for scholarships" and would seek to graduate at least one hundred black students over the five years.[57]

The law school dramatically exceeded that commitment. By 1971, only three years later, there were 110 black students enrolled. This represented almost 20 percent of the student body. By comparison, there were only about 800 black Rutgers University undergraduates out of 17,000, or less than 5 percent, and only 12 black students at Rutgers Law–Camden, or about 2 percent. By 1975, MSP applicants made up 513 of the 2,612 day school applicants, or nearly 20 percent.

The ABLS Indictment and the Tripartite Commission

Despite the considerable changes in curriculum, social consciousness and student diversity set in motion in 1968 and early 1969, the ABLS considered the changes inadequate. The increasing number of minority students actually seemed to heighten dissatisfaction with the curriculum. In the ABLS's view, despite some additional "relevant" courses, the curriculum still emphasized legal thinking over practice and was much more attuned to the representation of affluent people who were able to navigate the legal system.

On November 4, 1969, therefore, the ABLS published an "Indictment of the Rutgers Law School Community," calling for a complete overhaul of the law school curriculum. The statement addressed the relationship between legal education and all segments of society, and the ABLS demanded that the law school close down for a serious discussion of the issues raised by the indictment. At the top of the discussion agenda were the construction of a new curriculum and the development of a plan to attract more African American students and faculty. Among other things, the indictment criticized the virtual absence of courses relevant to trial practice, the scarcity of courses on criminal law and the absence of hands-on training. It stated its conclusion regarding the law school's curriculum in the following strong terms:

> *We conclude that a mere cursory examination of the curriculum forces one to realize that the private interests of white society are far more thoroughly protected by the curriculum than the private interests of Black people. It should also be noted, at this point, that even a narrow disparity between* [the interests that the curriculum protects] *cannot easily be brushed aside; for the negative effect of this disparity on equal protection under the law for Blacks is compounded when one takes into account that in most of*

these areas, the interests of Blacks and whites are adverse! White people are protecting acquired and vested property rights within a system of legal nepotism that forecloses most Blacks from entry. Black people are subject to the repressive tactics of those who would shout "law and order" to protect with [sic] interests from the envisioned threat of black emancipation. The curriculum at this law school is a violation of a Black person's rights to equal protection under the law.[58]

While the indictment specifically criticized the curriculum's failings as it affected black students and communities, similar criticisms could have been made on behalf of students from any disadvantaged community or those hoping to work on behalf these communities. The indictment provided an outline for change that included transforming all upper-class courses into clinics, in which the professor would maintain a docket of cases relevant to the course's subject matter and the students would assist in handling them.[59] It also demanded that unspecified courses be offered that were "relevant to Black students" and that these courses be taught by "Black instructors which are selected by the Black students in this law school."[60] The indictment dismissed the courses and seminars added by the law school in 1968 to aid underrepresented communities with a single observation: "We are also offered the debatable benefits of certain seminars such as Problems of the Urban Poor, Small Business Problems of the Urban Poor, and International Race Relations."[61]

On the day after the indictment was released, November 5, 1969, Rutgers Law did close for the day, during which the entire student body, faculty and administration considered the charges. This led to the establishment of the Tripartite Commission, composed of three black law students, three members of the Student Bar Association and three faculty members. Its goal was to address the allegations and demands of the ABLS indictment.

Six months later, on May 6, 1970, the Tripartite Commission published its "Strategy for Change," which proposed that the law school create a curriculum to address two realities of American society "by providing a legal education for those who would practice law on behalf of the traditional interests of society and those who would become 'a new breed of lawyers with deep roots in the honored past of our profession who [we] would characterize as people's lawyers.'"[62]

Some of the major changes were to adjust the curriculum, add a clinical education program serving the legal needs of the poor, establish a joint-degree curriculum with other colleges of Rutgers–Newark and create a research institute of which the law school would form an integral part. The law school also would train both para-professionals and sub-professionals to help with quasi-legal tasks in the community. Lastly, these changes were to be implemented immediately.

CURRICULAR CHANGES

The Tripartite Commission's report agreed with the indictment's charge regarding the inadequacy of the courses and seminars added in 1968: "[I]mpromptu, noninterrelated courses offered in any given semester by individual faculty members, consistent with their singular objectives, cannot be viewed as even an attempt to deal legitimately with the legal demands of contemporary society."[63] This recognition is one of many remarkable aspects of the school's response to the ABLS indictment. It effectively acknowledged that the school's curriculum for much of its history not only failed to address the interests of students like those who wrote the ABLS indictment but also could be seen as overtly hostile to them. For example, for years the school had offered a course called Creditor's Rights, a name clearly expressing an intention to prepare students to help lenders extract payment from borrowers, but it did not offer a course aimed at representing borrowers.

Against that backdrop, the "noninterelated courses," however inadequate they might have been, marked a dramatic shift in the years immediately prior to the indictment. Rutgers Law's willingness, nonetheless, to acknowledge that these seminars were unworthy of being called "even an attempt to deal legitimately with the legal demands of contemporary society" is striking.

The indictment, and the Tripartite Commission's response, resulted in dramatic changes in the law school curriculum. They included a major expansion of the incipient clinical program, the addition of Legal Representation of the Poor to the required first-year curriculum and the creation of small class sections for first-year courses. Every first-year student was to participate in one of these sections, where they would learn legal writing.[64]

The Tripartite Commission also stated that, during their second and third years of law school, students should be able to create their own courses of study. The commission proposed three curricular tracks, which included allowing students to follow the standard curriculum, specialize in urban studies or specialize in a particular area of law. The commission indicated that students could utilize "courses, clinics, and seminars" in order to make their education relevant to their goals.[65]

Except as noted here regarding casebooks, the commission did not especially focus on changing the content of continuing law school courses. Instead, it emphasized interdisciplinary studies—noting that the solutions to many problems faced by the urban poor required knowledge of other disciplines—and proposed new joint-degree programs focusing on these connections.[66] The commission did suggest that casebooks used in all subjects should be revised to ensure that they included materials relevant to urban problems, but it is unclear to what extent this was enacted.

On May 6, 1970, the same day that the report was published, the entire law school community voted to approve the "Strategy for Change." An Implementation Task Force was immediately created and began the difficult task of restructuring Rutgers Law to ensure that the desired changes would actually come to fruition.

In many respects, the changes made after the ABLS indictment and the Tripartite Commission's report put Rutgers at the cutting edge of legal education. Its clinical program, in particular, has been widely emulated. However, the ongoing courses offered seemed to change little if at all. Many of the relatively new public interest–oriented courses and seminars, found to be wholly inadequate by the indictment and the commission, were continued, and others were added over the years. Still, it was largely left to the burgeoning clinical programs and to the social justice efforts of individual faculty members, many in connection with the clinics and some independently, to address the core concerns of the ABLS and students with similar goals.

Succinctly capturing the period between 1970 and 1978 at Rutgers Law is extraordinarily difficult. It was a time of vast energy, enthusiasm and engagement. It was a time when many faculty members and students worked collaboratively to grapple with the great issues of the day: the growing opposition to a war that seemed to many ever more wasteful, hopeless and immoral; the growing belief that attention, energy and resources had to be devoted to curing the ills and gross inequalities within the United States; and the growing awareness that law and constitutional processes could be instrumental in achieving social and political justice here and abroad. It was a time when the challenges seemed great, but the potential for dealing with them seemed equally great.

Most of those who lived through the experience found it life- and career-altering. It was a time when Rutgers Law was widely known as the "People's

Electric Law School," and the late Professor John Payne became the main custodian of a T-shirt design with that appellation.

On the diversity front during those years, thanks to continuing strong support for the MSP, the black student population began to reach critical mass, and the first cohorts of MSP graduates began to make their marks on the legal profession and on the public life of New Jersey and the country. The faculty, too, began to creep toward greater diversity. The concept of diversity itself also broadened dramatically in terms of ethnicity and especially gender.

In 1970, Rutgers Law launched the *Women's Rights Law Reporter*, the first legal periodical in the country to focus exclusively on the field of women's legal rights. A dedicated and determined group of students worked with

Professor Ruth Bader Ginsburg.

Professor Ruth Bader Ginsburg to establish the *Reporter*. Its founding advisory board included many of the prominent female attorneys, academics and public figures in the country and one man—Professor Arthur Kinoy.

In 1973, Nadine Taub was appointed to the faculty to direct the Women's Rights Litigation Clinic. Under her leadership between 1973 and 2001, when she retired, the clinic was involved in path-breaking litigation regarding abortion, sterilization and other reproductive rights, as well as employment discrimination, including sexual harassment.

Professor Taub joined several female faculty members added to the Rutgers Law faculty between 1970 and 1973 to augment the two senior tenured women—Ginsburg and Eva Morreale Hanks. Annamay Sheppard joined the faculty in 1970 from the Newark Legal Services program and was instrumental in the establishment of the Urban Legal Clinic. Diana Sclar arrived in 1973 from an attorney's position with the U.S. Department of Housing and Urban Development.

In the student body, the early to mid-1970s were years of great growth in the number and percentage of women, and in 1977 Rutgers Law was reputedly the first law school in the country to have a majority of women.[67] Of the women in attendance, many were "mature," having returned to their own education after their children became full-day students. Their parenting responsibilities didn't cease, though, and they formed especially close relationships with one another because of their need for emotional and physical support. This led some of them later to call themselves the "Band of Mothers." Beyond the impressive advances between 1970 and 1978 in student and faculty diversity, Rutgers Law's clinical programs flourished. Early in that period, a student returned from a meeting at Harvard Law School flourishing a mimeographed poster he had received there. Styled after a football scoreboard, it read, "RUTGERS 86; HARVARD 3." That represented the number of credits of clinical programs available then at the two law schools.

Actually, Rutgers Law's clinical opportunities predated 1970. In the 1950s and even 1940s, students had "pre-clinical" opportunities—the chance to participate in the representation of people charged with relatively minor offenses.[68]

The *Rutgers Law Bulletin* for 1947–48 referred to an "experimental" legal practice clinic in the Essex County courts that offered students "a chance for real service to the criminal court" and "for valuable experience." Similar descriptions appeared in bulletins during the next several school years under the heading of "Legal Clinic."

By 1952–53, the reference to "experimental" was eliminated, and the heading became "Clinical Training." The description, and the program itself, was much broader: "Provision is made for the appointment of law students as junior counsel in cases in the criminal courts throughout the state to which counsel have been assigned to handle the cases of indigent persons charged with the commission of crimes."

This program continued into the mid-1960s, when a court rule was adopted expanding the clinical work that students could do. The rule permitted "qualified third-year students [to] represent indigent persons in the Small Claims Divisions of the County District Courts." Student representation of indigents in both criminal and civil matters continued in various forms at least through the early 1990s. For some of that time, it was referred to as the Rutgers Legal Aid Clinic, and beginning in the early 1970s, it functioned in cooperation with the Newark Legal Services Project. Longstanding as this "clinical" activity by law students was, however, it seemed to be done on a pro bono, non-credit basis.

The first Rutgers Law clinical venture for which students were awarded credit was established in 1968. In conjunction with the U.S. Equal Employment Opportunity Commission, with which Professor Alfred Blumrosen came to have close ties, and the New Jersey Division on Civil Rights, Blumrosen and his faculty colleagues Frank Askin and Richard Chused established the Administrative Process Project. For several years, faculty and students worked on state administrative regulations to promote both equal employment opportunities and fair housing access and issued reports about their efforts.[69]

Of Rutgers Law's early formal clinical programs, or at least those that have continued to the present, the Urban Legal Clinic may have responded most directly to the challenge of the ABLS indictment, providing direct legal services to members of the community in connection with landlord-tenant issues, domestic relations, employment and a range of other problems experienced by urban residents of modest means. Other early clinics sought to serve the community as well, but they tended to be relatively short-lived. These included the Juvenile Court Clinic, the Consumer Protection Clinic, the Health Rights Clinic, the Legal Rights of the Mentally Disabled Clinic and the Inmate Defender Clinic (which morphed into the Corrections Clinic and then the longer-running Prison Law Clinic).

By contrast, the Women's Rights Litigation Clinic dealt with a range of legal issues of special concern to women, and the Constitutional Litigation Clinic, for the most part, was the general-purpose "big case" clinic, handling

Professor Alfred Blumrosen at a Centennial event. *Courtesy of Shelley Kusnetz.*

a wide variety of cutting-edge cases involving the constitutional rights of citizens. It also often became the litigation home of faculty members with personal social justice agendas who were not formally attached to the clinical programs. Among others, Professor Paul Tractenberg's earliest school funding and educational reform litigation was done in conjunction with the Constitutional Litigation Clinic and a team of its students. Professor John Payne's landmark work on affordable housing in the Mount Laurel litigation was also done primarily in combination with the ConLit Clinic, as it came to be called.

One early ConLit Clinic case directly linked up to the Newark community and one of the underlying causes of the 1967 disorders. Those disorders revealed, if it had not been known before, that the Newark Police and Fire Departments substantially excluded African Americans and Hispanics from employment. In 1972, ConLit faculty and students filed federal class action lawsuits challenging racial and national origin discrimination that had kept minorities from being hired or promoted in both departments.[70] The lawsuits continued for a decade and a half, involving generations of Rutgers Law students, and were finally resolved at the end of the 1980s with substantial improvements in the departments' hiring and promotion practices, a substantial financial settlement for previously excluded police department candidates and other opportunities for the class of previously excluded applicants. The departments have been much more integrated ever since.

As a distinctive sidebar, the litigation went on long enough, and contributed to enough changes in the departments, that by the end one of the original plaintiffs in the police case—Officer Claude Coleman, president of the Bronze Shields police officer organization—had become the director of the Newark Fire Department and thus a defendant! Coleman also graduated from Rutgers Law in 1977, is now a Superior Court judge and in 1994, in a widely publicized story, was wrongfully arrested for theft and fraud in Bloomingdale's at the posh Short Hills Mall. In truth, Coleman's only offense seems to have been SWB ("shopping while black").

During the People's Electric Law School days of the 1970s, the atmosphere truly was electric—different than that of almost any other place faculty members or students ever experienced. Diversity and the commitment to using law to advance social justice were a substantial part of that special character, but it went beyond that.

Professor Tractenberg tells a story of his first teaching experience at Rutgers Law in 1970 in a large-enrollment course in Business Associations,

Professor Paul Tractenberg. *Courtesy of Shelley Kusnetz.*

the basic corporate law course. As a first-time teacher, he decided to canvass his 150 students about why they were taking the course and used a simple survey. He promised the students he would tabulate the result and report back to them. That evening, he discovered that fully one-third of the students said that they were taking the course so that they could destroy capitalism. His report the next day was short and to the point: those who wanted to destroy capitalism should learn corporate law better than those who wanted to defend capitalism.

Of course, even in the heady days of the People's Electric Law School, most students were at Rutgers Law to become good lawyers and engage in the profession in ways that would unfold in the future, perhaps in different directions than they expected. Yet many whose careers developed in seemingly traditional ways after their Rutgers Law experience have attested to the profound effect their exposure to diversity, commitment to social justice and, yes, even some political extremism had on their views.[71]

CHAPTER 5

THE TUMULTUOUS LATER YEARS (1978–2008)

Hanging On to the Magic or Reverting to Tradition
(The People's Electric Law School Short-Circuited or Recharged)

In many ways, 1978 was a watershed year for Rutgers Law. Sustaining the intensity of the 1960s and first part of the 1970s, and of the People's Electric Law School, seemed increasingly unlikely. In part, that was because the clinics and allied faculty had achieved some extraordinary litigation victories, establishing major new constitutional principles and rights in the late 1960s and early to mid-1970s, but the late 1970s also seemed a time of building on those lofty principles and rights to make them real. In litigation, as in much of life, implementation is much harder and less dramatic than establishing principles. So, Rutgers Law had to face a moment of truth—did it have the persistence to see its important work through to completion?

At the same time, there were national developments affecting higher education, and legal education in particular, and others waiting in the wings that would make this thirty-year concluding period in Rutgers Law's first one hundred years at least as challenging as any of the previous epochs. Rutgers Law's foundational commitments to diversity, to public service and public interest law and to curricular innovation, especially, in the form of law clinics, as well as its commitment to enhancing its status through a heightened emphasis on academic excellence, were all at risk during this period. Some of the buffeting threatened to have especially serious effects on Rutgers Law; others threatened to affect all public law schools.

It has to be said, though, that throughout its history Rutgers Law has sought to balance its special commitments against its general responsibility to provide an excellent program designed to prepare its graduates to practice law, often in small New Jersey firms. Over the years, that is what the bulk of

Rutgers Law alumni have done. And that is what Rutgers Law has sought to equip them to do well.

So, one important theme in the Rutgers Law story of 1978 to 2008 is how it has sought, in some very difficult times, to balance and make good on its potentially divergent but ultimately complementary responsibilities—to offer high-quality professional educational opportunities to those interested in all aspects of law while retaining its strong commitment to educating students to help the disadvantaged and underserved. The bottom line seems to be that to a remarkable degree, given its relatively small budget and faculty, Rutgers Law has largely managed to discharge those complex and sometimes competing responsibilities. Often, it has been a complicated and contentious juggling act, made far more difficult by challenges from outside and inside to some of its core principles and by changes in the broader world of legal education, perhaps most notably the advent in the mid-1990s of the *U.S. News & World Report*'s annual ranking of law schools.

This chapter will be organized around how Rutgers Law responded to challenges to its three transformative pillars—diversity; public interest and public service; and curricular innovation, especially through clinical legal education. It will then address the confounding effects of some broader changes in legal education and especially legal education in public law schools.

Challenging Diversity in Higher Education: First the *Bakke* Case and then the U.S. Office of Civil Rights

The first major challenge out of the gate struck at one of Rutgers Law's signature commitments: achieving diversity in its student body and in the legal profession. It took the form of a serious legal challenge to affirmative action in higher education.

Allan Bakke, a white male who was denied acceptance to the Medical School of the University of California at Davis, filed a lawsuit in the California state courts challenging the constitutionality of the school's special admissions program because he claimed that it operated to exclude him on the basis of race. Under that program, disadvantaged minority applicants competed against one another for designated seats in the entering class, with white applicants excluded from consideration for those seats. The California courts, culminating with the state supreme court, struck down the admissions program as violating the federal Equal Protection Clause because it was not the least intrusive means of achieving the Medical School's stated goals of integrating the medical profession and increasing the number of doctors willing to serve minority patients.

The U.S. Supreme Court agreed to hear the case, *Regents of the University of California v. Bakke*,[72] and by the time the case reached the court in 1977, it had generated a firestorm of controversy and debate. No fewer than thirty-eight amici curiae (friends of the court) briefs were submitted, twenty-eight supporting the constitutionality of the University of California–Davis special admissions program. Included among the twenty-eight were briefs submitted by the United States, the State of Washington, many of the nation's leading civil rights organizations, many of the leading organizations involved in medical and legal education, a number of important universities and law schools, several bar associations and organizations of black law students from three law schools.

It was hardly surprising, given Rutgers Law's leadership role in promoting affirmative action, that Professors Annamay Sheppard and Jonathan Hyman filed a brief on behalf of the Rutgers Board of Governors, the Law School Alumni Association and the Student Bar Association. They were aided on the brief by Professor Arthur Kinoy and many law students enrolled in both the Affirmative Action Seminar and the Constitutional Litigation Clinic. Adding to Rutgers Law's representation before the court were Professor Frank Askin and former professor Ruth Bader Ginsburg. They were part of the legal team that submitted a brief on behalf of the American Civil Liberties Union.

In the spring of 1978, a sharply divided U.S. Supreme Court rendered its decision, affirming the California Supreme Court decision in part and also reversing it in part. The court ruled that racial quotas or set-asides, such as those employed in UC–Davis's special admissions program, were impermissible but that race could be considered as a "plus factor" in an otherwise racially neutral process. The *Bakke* decision clearly was a landmark, generating more national attention than any litigation about racial discrimination since *Brown v. Board of Education* almost a quarter century earlier.[73] However, the intricacies of *Bakke*'s multiple opinions and the complexities of the justices' alignment defied easy understanding.

Uncertainty about the scope and reach of this decision led many schools, including many law schools, to scale back or even eliminate their affirmative action admissions programs. Rutgers Law was determined not to reflexively take that approach. It understood that it faced a moment of truth. Was it sufficiently committed to diversity at the school and in the profession to continue its MSP, or should it join other schools and scale back?

By the spring of 1978, when *Bakke* was decided, Rutgers Law's MSP had grown to include approximately 25 percent of each entering class. The *Bakke* decision put it in the spotlight and provoked a serious, sometimes heated, discussion about it. There were sharp divisions in the Rutgers Law community about how the school should proceed. Some thought that *Bakke* had signaled that the MSP program would be deemed unconstitutional and argued that it should be altered before then. Others believed that the MSP could pass constitutional muster even after *Bakke*. A lawsuit actually was filed challenging the MSP, but it was dismissed on technical grounds and never decided on the merits.[74]

Meanwhile, the school received many communications from both former students and community groups overwhelmingly extolling the virtues of the program and urging its continuation. On the other side were legal evaluations of the MSP, solicited from several area law firms, which opined that the program was unconstitutional. Clearly, Rutgers Law, and its strong commitment to diversity, stood at a crossroads.

Seeking to create an informed basis for action, both the law school's Admissions Committee and Minority Student Program Committee were convened to evaluate the *Bakke* decision and its likely impact on Rutgers Law's special admission program. In particular, the focus was on the admissions process for the class to enter in the fall of 1979.

The MSP Committee's unanimous position throughout was that Rutgers Law's special admissions program was consistent with the *Bakke* decision. The members noted that the medical school whose program was challenged in *Bakke* made no effort to demonstrate that its past admissions policies and practices had a discriminatory effect. By contrast, the MSP Committee pointed out that Rutgers Law's 1972 announcement on admissions had acknowledged that its reliance on traditional admissions criteria had resulted in the virtual exclusion of minority students. In the committee's view, this clearly distinguished the law school's program from the program invalidated in *Bakke*.

The MSP Committee's position was reflected in a lengthy brief prepared by the Constitutional Law Clinic and distributed to the faculty and to the broader law school community. According to an introduction to the *Rutgers Law Review*'s compilation of documents relating to the faculty debates about *Bakke*, the brief had two purposes: "to persuade the faculty not to weaken the program and to demonstrate that a convincing legal defense could be presented were the program challenged in court."[75]

The admissions committee, chaired by Professor Sheppard, was more reflective of the divergent opinions of the faculty as a whole. The four faculty members divided evenly on the question of whether the faculty should vote to maintain the MSP in its current form.

Professors Sheppard and Hyman favored maintenance—not a surprise given their joint authorship of the friend-of-the-court brief submitted to the U.S. Supreme Court in *Bakke*.

Professors Norman Cantor and Alan Schwarz, both constitutional law teachers, questioned the constitutionality of the MSP and favored a "diversity model" with a minority student goal of 20 percent. Under their recommended model, the admissions process would be unitary rather than dual, as was true of the MSP, with all applicants evaluated by the same law school reviewer, probably the admissions director. The notion of "diversity" would be expanded beyond race and ethnicity to include gender, age and economic and educational disadvantage. A percentage goal would be established for each diversity group, with the Cantor-Schwarz illustrative percentages given as "at least" 20 percent women, 10 percent "older" students (at least five years out of college), 10 percent economically and educationally disadvantaged students (a precise definition to be formulated) and 20 percent minority students.[76] Cantor and Schwarz recognized that there were many questions and many fine-tuning points regarding their model.

However, it must be said in the strongest terms that no member of the faculty spoke in favor of eliminating Rutgers Law's historic commitment to diversity in its student body or in the legal profession. Rather, differences of opinion related to constitutional analysis and, given that analysis, how a constitutionally defensible program should be formulated.

The admissions committee did far more than have an in-house debate. Among other things, it conducted five days of open public hearings in October 1978 and received many written statements to supplement the oral testimony. A wide array of organizations was represented at the hearings, including the NAACP, the Garden State Bar Association (an association of black lawyers), the Association of Black Women Lawyers of New Jersey, the Urban League of Essex County, the National Lawyers Guild, the Committee Against Racism, the Puerto Rican Congress of New Jersey, the Asian American Legal Defense and Education Fund, the Puerto Rican Legal Defense Fund, the Rutgers Law Student Bar Association, the Asian-American Law Students, the Association of Black Law Students, the Association of Latin American Law Students, the Pacific-Asian Coalition

(NJIT) and the Rutgers Women's Caucus. Among the individuals speaking were Newark's Mayor Kenneth Gibson; former Rutgers Law dean Heckel; and Judge Betty Lester, a 1971 graduate of the law school.[77]

The admissions committee included five student members with voting rights, and they broke the faculty deadlock decisively. All voted in favor of the Sheppard-Hyman position, which thereupon became the committee's majority position and the basis for its report to the faculty.

The faculty engaged in an extended discussion of the report, with meetings, some of them open to the broader community, extending over a period of weeks.[78] Faculty members who participated have clear recollections of extensive media coverage of some of the public sessions.

Overhanging the faculty debate was concern that the university board of governors might consider altering or even rescinding its delegation of authority to the law school regarding the admission of students. For a considerable time, little consensus emerged about either the legality of the MSP or the morality of any of the proposed courses of action. At one point, this led to a proposal to seek an opinion from the U.S. Department of Health, Education and Welfare.

The issue was then debated before the entire Rutgers Law community at an open faculty meeting, much like the community discussion of the Tripartite Committee report ten years earlier in 1969. The competing arguments about constitutionality and policy were passionate, even heated. Some maintained that the MSP would survive constitutional challenge and that the school should make that clear. Others thought that discretion was the better part of valor and that the program should be altered in ways that would make it immune to serious challenge. No one argued for the elimination of affirmative action in admissions.

The proposal that carried the day was made by one of the black faculty members, himself a Rutgers Law graduate who helped, both as a student and faculty member, to shape the MSP originally. Professor Alfred Slocum, later to become the public advocate of New Jersey, recommended that the MSP should be enlarged, not scaled back, by adding to those eligible for it disadvantaged white applicants. By doing so, Slocum argued, we would eliminate the racial and ethnic character of the MSP. In effect, we would redefine the word "minority" in the MSP without changing the program's proud and well-known name. Interestingly, this idea seemed quite like an aspect of the Schwarz-Cantor dissent to the Admissions Committee report.

After the elaborate run-up to the decisive faculty vote, it occurred at a meeting "remarkable for its brevity and lack of discussion."[79] Presumably, the discussion had already occurred at prior meetings and in the corridors. By a vote of thirty-four to three, the faculty adopted the following resolution:

> *That the current Minority Student Program be expanded to 30%* [of the entering class] *and that the term "minority" be understood to include disadvantaged whites.*

At a later meeting, by an equally lopsided vote, thirty-three to two, the faculty adopted a detailed definition of "disadvantaged whites," the gist being that such applicants would have to demonstrate poverty or other educationally disadvantaging characteristics.

In this revised and expanded form, the MSP continued to be a defining attribute of Rutgers Law, affording generations of students of color and students with socioeconomic and educational disadvantages opportunities to attend law school and enter the legal profession. Literally thousands have seized those opportunities, changing the face of the profession and making a huge impact. At latest count, Rutgers Law has graduated more than 2,500 students of color who passed through the MSP. The great bulk of them have become members of the New Jersey Bar or other state bars. Currently, Rutgers Law's student body has about 37 percent people of color, as well as 43 percent women, showing no slackening of the school's commitment to diversity.[80]

For this to be accomplished, however, Rutgers Law had to overcome another challenge to its diversity commitment. The later challenge—almost twenty years after *Bakke*—came from a surprising quarter: the Office of Civil Rights (OCR) in the Clinton administration's Department of Education.

In May 1997, acting on a complaint, OCR sent a letter to the university raising questions and concerns about the MSP. OCR's representatives basically indicated in subsequent meetings that they liked Rutgers Law's diversity results, but that, in their judgment, the dual admissions process by which the results were achieved was legally suspect and had to be changed. That led to another extensive internal process at Rutgers Law though one not as public as the post-*Bakke* process almost twenty years earlier. After all, the context was different here—it was related to an ongoing administrative agency investigation and not the response to a published decision of the United States Supreme Court.

The Rutgers Law dean, Roger Abrams, responded to the OCR investigation by asking the MSP standing committee to initiate a review during the 1997–98 academic year. In November 1998, early in the next academic year, the faculty unanimously constituted an augmented MSP Committee with six faculty members—the four members of the MSP Committee and the chairs of the Admissions, Curriculum and Policy Committee and the Planning and Budget Committee—to carry the review forward. The faculty's charge to this MSP study committee was

> [t]o undertake a review of the procedures, operation, and outcomes of the Minority Student Program (MSP) and, where appropriate, the general admissions process, and to gather information about comparable programs elsewhere, with the purpose of examining the current goals of the MSP and whether the current structure is appropriate to achieve those goals or any changes in the program are advisable; and to report its findings and recommendations to the Faculty by September 30, 1999.[81]

Professors Charles Jones and Paul Tractenberg were named as co-chairs of the study committee, and its membership included other senior faculty members who had played important roles in the MSP's creation—Al Slocum and Al Blumrosen.

Additionally, four senior administrators were assigned to staff the committee but wound up being de facto members. Four law students were annexed to the committee as advisers but could not serve as members because of the confidentiality of many of the records the committee would be reviewing. Finally, the committee was authorized to consult with two external legal counsel retained by the university to handle the pending OCR matter (one a Rutgers Law MSP graduate who had become a distinguished partner at a leading New Jersey law firm), as well as with other outside educational, statistical, diversity and legal experts.

As with the immediate post-*Bakke* deliberations, there were sharply divergent views about how Rutgers Law should respond to this latest challenge to its diversity program. However, judicial decisions since *Bakke* had shifted the center of gravity somewhat.

The MSP had undeniably been a dual admissions system, with one track for "regular" admissions and a second for MSP applicants. In other words, the MSP was both an admissions system and a post-admission academic and social support program for MSP-admitted students. To a larger number of faculty members than previously, the legal doctrine seemed increasingly to call into question whether there was any supportable form of dual admissions system. Some still argued for retaining and defending the MSP as it had been implemented, but that proved to be a relatively sparsely held minority view.

The main focus then turned to what kind of modifications might preserve the core of the MSP, and its capacity to produce impressive diversity, while eliminating the dual admissions approach. In effect, the special MSP study committee was given three charges: (1) to eliminate the MSP's dual approach; (2) to maintain or even improve the student diversity achieved by the MSP; and (3) to maintain or even improve the average LSAT scores and UGPA of the entering students. Such numerical indicators had assumed greater prominence starting in 1994 when *U.S. News & World Report* launched its annual law school rankings.

To many, the study committee's assignment seemed to be an impossible mission. One of the ways in which the committee approached its assignment, however, was by engaging a prominent statistical expert from the Mellon Foundation to crunch numbers to determine whether there were unitary admissions systems that might satisfy both the diversity and numerical indicators benchmarks the committee had been given.

That was only one part of the committee's multifaceted approach, though. It also entertained out-of-the-box suggestions. For example, Professor Blumrosen, in a partial dissent from the committee report, urged that the faculty abandon the LSAT as an admissions criterion for a substantial part of the admissions pool. His reasoning was that, because LSAT scores correlated so strongly with race, ethnicity and socioeconomic status, substantial reliance on such scores would make the achievement of diversity virtually impossible. He also asserted that the predictive power of the LSAT was strongest at the extremes—those scoring highest and lowest on it. He therefore urged that the LSAT should be used to screen in those scoring at the upper end and exclude from admission those scoring below a certain level. As to the great bulk of the applicants in between, they should be admitted based entirely on an individualized evaluation of their personal characteristics and experience, criteria long used by Rutgers Law to supplement the LSAT for all applicants and especially for MSP applicants.

In effect, Professor Blumrosen argued that an admissions approach like the MSP's should be extended to many other applicants without regard to their race, ethnicity or socioeconomic status. That recommendation, though Professor Blumrosen pressed it as hard as he could before the committee and the entire faculty, did not carry the day.[82]

In Professor Slocum's dissent—a brilliant exegesis on the history, purpose and effect of the MSP—he made an argument similar to the one he had made in 1979: that we continue the MSP in its current form and face down the OCR challenge rather than succumb to a federal agency's politically motivated pressure. After all, he stressed, the MSP had been challenged several times in court and had never been found wanting.

Professor Slocum's main objection to the committee report—the plurality report in his terminology presumably because the four students working with the committee had not been given voting status and, if they had, would not have voted for it—is effectively captured by the following statement:

> *The major criticism of this proposal is quite frankly that it is, first and foremost, deceitful if the stipulated goals are to be believed* [that it is designed to achieve meaningful student diversity]. *A spade should be called a spade and race based admissions should be called just that. We should beware of Trojan horses such as* [are] *offered here. There is either going to be a concerted effort to rectify in some small measure the discriminating effects of the Great American paradigm* [of racism] *or there is not.*[83]

Professor Slocum's passionate argument had less traction with the faculty in 1999 than it had had in 1979, however, because of a strong perception that the legal landscape had changed significantly.

The report of the study committee, to which both Professors Blumrosen and Slocum took exception, essentially recommended a "unitary process with a single Admissions Committee considering all applicants and making all admissions decisions." In making those decisions, the "Admissions Committee shall be guided by a single set of admissions criteria applicable to all applicants" specifically set forth in a two-and-a-half-page-long appendix to the report. To achieve Rutgers Law's admissions goals, it was necessary to include among the criteria "race, ethnicity, socioeconomic circumstance, educational circumstance, disability and other factors" reflecting extraordinary circumstances or accomplishments. Given Rutgers Law's history, location and urban-oriented public service mission, the "Admissions Committee should pay special attention to application evidence of activities and accomplishments centering on the improvement of urban life and conditions." In making its decisions, the Admissions Committee should "not apply [the set of criteria] as a rigid point system." Finally, the Minority Student Program should be designated as the "MSP" and should function as a post-admission program, continuing, or even expanding, "the support and enrichment initiatives of the current Minority Student Program."[84]

At an extraordinary series of meetings in October and November 1999, the faculty sought to deal with the committee's recommendations and the competing views of Professors Blumrosen and Slocum. At a regular faculty meeting on October 28, the committee made an introductory presentation of the main features of the report against the backdrop of a review of the current admissions process.

On the morning of Tuesday, November 16,[85] at a meeting open to the Rutgers Law community, the faculty spent over two hours hearing and discussing a series of presentations, which drew the "battle lines." Professor Jones presented the highlights of the previously distributed majority report. Professor Blumrosen presented his minority report on the reduced use of the LSAT. Five law students presented their view that the MSP should be retained in its current form.

Two days later, on Thursday, November 18, the faculty reconvened, again initially at an open meeting, for more than two additional hours to continue the discussion. The record was augmented by memoranda submitted by the Student Bar Association. After general discussion, the faculty moved into executive session, with four students, designated by the SBA, in attendance.

After general discussion, the executive session was adjourned for two more days, until Saturday, November 20, when it was reconvened at 9:15 a.m. and continued until 5:10 p.m.[86] At the outset, there was yet another addition to the record: a memorandum from alumni, distributed to the faculty, expressing both concerns about the process triggered by OCR and support for the MSP.

After a wide-ranging but general discussion about the proposed revisions to the MSP and their implications, there was a suggestion that the discussion focus on three options: (1) the committee's proposal; (2) the Blumrosen proposal; and (3) continuation of the existing MSP. When put to a nonbinding straw vote, the committee's proposal garnered more than 70 percent and the other two slightly less than 15 percent each.

As a result, the meeting turned to a discussion of the committee's proposal. The discussion produced many suggestions and several motions about relatively peripheral issues. On the central question, though, of whether the committee's proposal should supplant the dual admissions system, including the MSP, the faculty seemed deadlocked.

Midway through the afternoon, after the meeting had been going on for about six hours, Professor Tractenberg proposed an outside-the-box solution—which was actually more of an inside-the-box solution. As the faculty minutes reflect, because Tractenberg could not speak as a result of a sore throat, MSP dean Janice Robinson made the motion on his behalf. It was to have the application configured so that every applicant could check a box indicating that he or she wished to be reviewed on primarily nonnumerical factors, an option previously available only to applicants for MSP admission.

The faculty approved that amendment to the committee's proposal, and eventually the proposal as so amended was overwhelmingly adopted with only one negative vote and three abstentions. The faculty, however, rejected the committee's recommendation that the official name of the program be changed from the Minority Student Program to the MSP.

The effect was to replace the dual admissions system with a unitary one under which a single Admissions Committee would consider all applicants under an explicit single set of criteria. Under that unitary system, however, every applicant could choose to be reviewed with greater or lesser weight given to numerical and nonnumerical factors. The MSP would cease to be an admissions system but would continue as a post-admission support and enrichment program. Finally, the new admissions system was subject to a three-year sunset provision; it could not be employed beyond three years unless the faculty acted to continue it in the same or a modified form.

This new system was implemented through a series of boxes on the Rutgers Law application. The first two dealt with which criteria—numerical (i.e., LSAT and UGPA) or nonnumerical (i.e., personal experiences and accomplishments)—were to be given primary emphasis. The other box related to whether the applicant wished to participate in the MSP as a post-admission support program.

That admissions system has been in effect since it was adopted by the faculty in November 1999, having been reviewed and approved in 2002. To the great satisfaction and relief of most, it has enabled Rutgers Law to meet OCR's legal concerns at the same time that it has yielded diversity and numerical indicators at least as high as they were prior to 1998. By way of illustration, from 2003 until 2009 between 35 percent and 41 percent of Rutgers Law's total enrollment were students of color, and during that same period between 33 percent and 43 percent of the school's graduates were students of color. Ironically, it was not until July 2008 that OCR formally notified Rutgers University that it had closed the matter. Thus, during the period between 1978 and 2008, Rutgers Law twice faced down major challenges to its diversity commitment. Strikingly, in both situations it found creative ways to preserve the substance of its commitment to diversity while advancing other institutional interests.

That is not to say that the effort has been cost-free or that the changes adopted have not generated concerns and even ill feeling, especially among those who were products of the original MSP and have a deep emotional attachment to it. Nor is it to say that Rutgers Law's core commitment to affirmative action and diversity, whatever form it has taken, has been immune from criticism, often as a result of misinformation.

Moreover, the state of the law is still shifting, with the U.S. Supreme Court's 2003 decisions in the University of Michigan affirmative action cases *Grutter* (sustaining the law school's admissions process[87]) and *Gratz* (invalidating the undergraduate admission process[88]) and in the Supreme Court's more recent decision in the *Parents Involved* case, striking down two K–12 voluntary affirmative action policies.[89] Additionally, state constitutional amendments have been proposed, and in some cases adopted, to bar the use of racial preferences in higher education admissions. As a consequence, Rutgers Law may be called on, once again, to respond to a challenge to its diversity commitment.

For the moment, though, the new admissions system has stood the test of time regarding student diversity, numerical indicators and legality, and the MSP remains a vital force at Rutgers Law, although it has assumed a different form. The diversity bottom line is that Rutgers Law continues to be one of the most diverse law schools in the nation, located on a campus—Rutgers–Newark—that has been ranked by *USNWR* for each of the thirteen years it has done such a ranking as the most diverse national university campus. The latest report gives Rutgers–Newark a diversity index of 0.74, meaning that "nearly 3 out of every 4 people you run into there will be from a different ethnic group."[90]

Between the late 1960s, when Rutgers Law was an overwhelmingly white male law school, and 2008, the school radically transformed itself and the legal profession it serves. Over that period, it has graduated more than 2,500 people of color and a comparable number of women, many of whom have become prominent leaders of bench and bar. The following are among the most prominent examples but are only a small sampling of those worthy of recognition:

- Elizabeth Warren, '76, Leo Gottlieb Professor of Law at Harvard University, and chair of the Congressional Oversight Panel, which has responsibility for reviewing "the current state of financial markets and the regulatory system," including the $700 billion Troubled Asset Relief Program.
- U.S. Senator Robert Menendez, '79.
- Ronald Chen, '83, public advocate of New Jersey (Stanley Van Ness, '63, was the first public advocate; Zulima Farber, '74, and Alfred Slocum, '70, also served in the position).

- Yvonne Smith Segars, '84, public defender of New Jersey.
- Jennifer Velez, '96, commissioner, New Jersey Department of Human Services.
- Virginia Long, '66, and Jaynee LaVecchia, '79, associate justices of the New Jersey Supreme Court.
- Wade Henderson, '73, president and CEO, Leadership Conference on Civil Rights.
- Hazel Rollins O'Leary, '66, president, Fisk University, and former U.S. secretary of energy.
- Ida Castro, '82, vice-president of Social Justice and Diversity, Commonwealth Medical College, and former chairwoman, U.S. Equal Employment Opportunity Commission.
- Hubert Williams, '74, president, Police Foundation.
- Ann Lesk, '77, partner, Fried Frank, and president, New York County Lawyers' Association.
- Candice Beinecke, '70, chair, Hughes, Hubbard & Reed.
- Margaret Pfeiffer, '74, first woman to become a partner at Sullivan & Cromwell.
- Patricia Nachtigal, '76, managing attorney, Ingersoll-Rand.
- Zulima Farber, '74, partner, Lowenstein Sandler; first Hispanic woman to serve as a member of New Jersey governor's cabinet as public advocate; and former attorney general of New Jersey.
- Sybil Moses, '74, first woman to become an assignment judge in New Jersey judicial system.
- Marilyn Morheuser, '73, former executive director, Education Law Center, and chief counsel for plaintiffs in *Abbott v. Burke.*
- Alfred Slocum, '70, Professor Emeritus, Rutgers Law, and former public advocate of New Jersey.
- Vincent Warren, '93, executive director, Center for Constitutional Rights.
- Donna Lieberman, '73, executive director, New York Civil Liberties Union.

Keeping the Public Interest and Public Service Flame Alive

It was probably inevitable that the intensity of the People's Electric Law School could not be maintained. Partly it was a function of changing times, changing circumstances and a changing public and political dynamic. Partly it was a result of some major inspirational figures leaving Rutgers Law during this last thirty-year period of Rutgers Law's first one hundred years. Ruth Bader Ginsburg, who had been an early champion of women's rights, actually left the faculty a bit earlier, in 1972. Nadine Taub, who picked up the mantle of leadership from Justice Ginsburg in 1973, herself retired in 2001. Annamay Sheppard, who was a central figure in both the creation of the Urban Legal Clinic and the fight to preserve the MSP, retired in 1999. Willard Heckel, the only dean in Rutgers Law's modern history to have graduated from the school and a towering figure in the 1960s and 1970s in the school and in the broader community, retired in 1983.

If there was one Rutgers Law figure who symbolized more than any other the People's Electric Law School, it was Arthur Kinoy. Combining constitutional creativity, charisma and almost messianic fervor, he left a huge imprint on Rutgers Law, far bigger than his diminutive stature might have suggested. He retired, actually unwillingly, in 1992 when he became seventy, at that time the mandatory retirement age. His continuing impact on the school is reflected, at least symbolically, by the fact that one of the law school computer servers is still designated as "kinoy.rutgers.edu."

Rutgers Law faculty and students continue to do enormously important public interest work, and major new faculty members have joined the school to lead the way. One of them, Eric Neisser, died tragically at much too early an age, but he left a great legacy, and the public interest center at Rutgers Law appropriately bears his name.

Some of the recent public interest and law reform work is path-breaking. Much of it continues to be centered in the Constitutional Legal Clinic, under the co-direction of Frank Askin, its founder, and Penny Venetis. Askin's continuing work on First Amendment rights and Venetis's work on two fronts—having U.S. courts recognize and apply international human rights norms and assuring the accuracy and security of voting machines— are widely recognized and applauded.

There's yet another reason why the atmosphere of Rutgers Law is not as intensely infused with the excitement of the People's Electric Law School, though. A number of important and exciting public interest law reform breakthroughs were achieved in the 1970s and 1980s. Since then, the efforts have continued, but they have been focused more on the implementation of important doctrinal principles and rights than on the establishment of new doctrine and rights. Implementation is almost always more frustrating and less exciting, especially when implementation is halting or inadequate to truly enforce the doctrinal rights.

Professor Frank Askin. *Courtesy of Bill Blanchard.*

Here are two important examples of many. One is the four-decade-long effort to reform the funding and educational programs of New Jersey's urban public schools. The other is the almost-as-longstanding effort to provide affordable housing in every region of the state.

In the first case, *Abbott v. Burke*[91] (and its predecessor, *Robinson v. Cahill*[92]), the litigation has been going on almost continuously since 1970. Professor Tractenberg—initially through his Public Education Law seminar and the Constitutional Litigation Clinic and since 1973 through the Education Law Center, a public interest law project he founded—has been involved throughout. Especially in the early years, Rutgers Law students have been actively engaged in the case.

A team of students representing both the seminar and the Constitutional Litigation Clinic played a central role in developing a major brief to the New Jersey Supreme Court in 1972. The brief, on behalf of two amici curiae—the ACLU of New Jersey and the NAACP Newark chapter education committee—argued that the state constitution's education clause, the centerpiece of the litigation ever since, should be construed to assure students in poor urban school districts the highest quality education possible. One of the law students who worked on that brief was Donna Lieberman, '73, now the executive director of the New York Civil Liberties Union.

In the *Abbott* stage of the litigation, that position was effectively adopted by the court when it ruled that the funding benchmark for students in the so-called "Abbott districts," the thirty-one poor urban districts, should be the average expenditure in the state's wealthiest and most successful suburban districts plus additional funding to meet the urban students' special needs and renovate or replace all deficient school buildings. Moreover, the court ruled that those students had to be provided with high-quality, well-planned early childhood education starting at age three if they were to have a meaningful opportunity to receive the constitutional education described as "thorough and efficient."

Since 1998, when *Abbott* began to be almost fully implemented, court-mandated state funding of the poor urban districts has amounted to billions of dollars per year, and there is compelling evidence that Abbott funding and the education reforms required to be provided with it have begun to enhance educational outcomes and reduce achievement gaps among urban and suburban students.[93] Those accomplishments are incomplete and uneven, however, as one would expect from ten years of serious efforts to reverse decades of educational neglect, coupled with the broader social and economic disadvantages confronted by most students in New Jersey's poor urban communities.

The implementation stage has engaged the advocates and the court in the nitty-gritty of school governance and programmatic reform for more than ten years. Important as it is to hundreds of thousands of New Jersey students, it's not the stuff of high drama. Some would say that lawyers and courts should not even be involved.

Then there's the unpredictable effect of external circumstances: the economy, the political climate and new educational panaceas. These can undermine the most diligent implementation efforts, especially when they arise at the same time.

New Jersey is at such a crossroads now. In May 2009, the New Jersey Supreme Court issued the *Abbott XX*[94] decision (yes, that means twenty decisions in just the *Abbott* phase of this litigation), which changed the implementation landscape by upholding, at least for the moment, a new school funding law that eliminates the favored treatment of the thirty-one Abbott districts and instead directs state funding to "at-risk" students wherever they attend public school. By September 1, 2010, the state commissioner of education must evaluate the statute's effect, and its constitutionality "as applied" will hinge on that evaluation.

Further complicating implementation is the election of Republican Christopher Christie as governor and the budget crisis he will confront. With a multibillion-dollar deficit projected, a balanced budget mandate and state aid for education as far and away the largest line item in the state budget, it is hard to imagine that Christie will not entertain ways to reduce such aid. But shifting more of the education cost burden onto the state's already desperately overburdened local property tax base doesn't seem viable. Perhaps Christie's avowed support of school choice will enter the picture as a possible cost-saving measure.

Ultimately, how these possibilities play out is likely to wind up yet again before the New Jersey Supreme Court. But the court's composition and likely role is in the hands of the new governor. During his first term, Christie will get to replace two of the seven New Jersey Supreme Court justices, who must step down at the mandatory retirement age of seventy, and he will get to re-nominate or replace two others.

The intricacies of this situation should dramatize why the implementation stage of public interest law reform litigation is so much more complex, stressful and less dramatic than the stage at which important new principles are articulated.

New Jersey's almost equally long effort to ensure affordable housing throughout the state—usually referred to as the *Mount Laurel* litigation[95]— reveals another face of implementation's challenges. This is another case closely linked to Rutgers Law. The late Professor John Payne, members of the clinical faculty and many students over the years were heavily engaged in various aspects of the effort.

Unlike school funding, though, most would acknowledge that *Mount Laurel* has never had the kind of measurable impact that *Abbott* achieved. That may have something to do with the underlying constitutional principles, or it may have more to do with the court's unwillingness to play the kind of long-term and prescriptive role it did in *Abbott*. In *Mount Laurel*, the court not only spoke of deference to the other branches, as it did repeatedly in *Abbott*, but it also actually deferred at crucial stages of the litigation when giving effective force to the constitutional principle was at stake. As a consequence, strong political forces were able to influence how both the legislative and executive branches responded.

One might well say that this is as it should be under our system of separation of powers and limited judicial powers to intervene. Yet in *Abbott*, the New Jersey Supreme Court spoke directly of its role as the "last resort guarantor of constitutional rights" and acted accordingly. In *Mount Laurel*, that theme was far more muted, if it was meaningfully present at all, perhaps attributable to the difference in the strength of the basic constitutional right at stake.

Staying at the Curricular Cutting Edge or Regaining It: The Clinics and the Broader Curriculum

The third dimension of Rutgers Law's transformation in the late 1960s and early 1970s—in addition to diversity and public interest law reform—was on the curricular front. Most dramatic was the initiation of the clinical program, but there were other potentially far-reaching curricular changes. Staying at the cutting edge or regaining it in both areas is yet another major challenge for Rutgers Law.

Clinics

By 1978, legal clinics were firmly established at Rutgers Law. In 2008, they continue to be.[96] Yet, the intervening three decades saw important changes, shifts in orientation, difficult intra-faculty issues and changes in national repute.

Two mainstays of the clinical program—the Constitutional Litigation Clinic and the Urban Clinic—were in place from 1970 and continue at the heart of our clinics. They were augmented in the early 1970s by the

The Center for Law and Justice.

Women's Rights Litigation Clinic, which has been inactive since 2006. These three early clinics followed a similar model—headed by a tenured or tenure-track faculty member assigned to the clinic and supported by one or more staff attorneys.

By 1974, the Prison Law Clinic was added to the mix, but it followed a somewhat different model—a tenure-track faculty member was associated with the clinic while teaching a full-time nonclinical load, but an adjunct faculty member was the mainstay. Still, the Prison Law Clinic, which drew much of its caseload from the ACLU's Prisoners' Rights Organized Defense project, remained in operation until 1990. By contrast, a Labor Law Clinic added in 1980 and staffed by two adjuncts lasted only two years. A Mental Health Law Clinic, also staffed by adjuncts, had a comparably short tenure.

In 1985, a major new clinical enterprise—the Environmental Law Clinic—entered the picture, and it followed yet another, if shifting, model. It was heavily funded by the Eastern Environmental Law Center and for much of its twenty-four-year tenure at the law school functioned more as a public interest law project or an in-house externship than as a traditional law school clinical program. Since the spring of 2009, the project has continued to function in Newark as the Eastern Environmental Law Center but located in a downtown office building separate from the law school. A tenure-track faculty member hired to direct the clinic, only to find it no longer at the law school, is exploring avenues for reconstituting the program in a different and smaller format.

The Animal Rights Clinic began to operate in 1990, and it reverted to the earlier clinical model of a tenured faculty member directing and a staff attorney assisting. It functioned until 2000.

A Women and AIDS Clinic was spun off from the Women's Rights Litigation Clinic in the late 1990s and became fully independent in 1999. Its focus was on an urban population group particularly ravaged by the HIV/ AIDS epidemic, and therefore it was clearly responsive to the Tripartite Commission's call for the law school's engagement with the local community. This clinic ceased operating in 2004 when its director left Rutgers Law.

More recently, four additional clinics—the Community Law Clinic, the Federal Tax Law Clinic, the Child Advocacy Clinic and the Special Education Clinic—were added. That leaves six fully operating clinics and one—the Environmental Law Clinic—going through a restructuring process. The shifts in Rutgers Law's clinical education programs over the past thirty years were about much more than the precise alignment of clinics, though. They involve status within the school and in the broader world of legal education and the nature of the clinical enterprise itself.

In 1978, Rutgers Law was still very much at the cutting edge of clinical legal education in the United States. The program, like the MSP in diversity, was widely regarded as a pioneering venture, one admired and emulated by other law schools. In 2008, Rutgers Law's clinical education program was large, diverse and prominent but no longer distinctive. A substantial number of other law schools have caught up to Rutgers Law and in some cases eclipsed it, at least in the size of their clinical enterprises.

There are two primary reasons: first, relative to other law schools, especially those in the New York City metropolitan area, Rutgers Law's clinical program has suffered, as have other aspects of the school, from declining resources; second, paradoxically, the clinical program has been a victim of its early success. Due to the accomplishments of law schools like ours, the ABA now requires all law schools to offer their students live-client experiential learning opportunities, and virtually all of the nearly two hundred accredited law schools now have clinical programs as a result.

The challenge for the future is to try to find a way to recapture the widely acknowledged leadership role Rutgers Law once had in clinical legal education and to do so, at least for the time being, with a diminishing clinical faculty, staff and resources relative to many other law schools.

That's not to suggest, however, that things have been static during those three decades or that, by most benchmarks, Rutgers Law's clinical programs aren't still outstanding. There have been a number of major changes. One has to do with the status of clinical faculty. Indeed, even referring to them as "faculty" suggests a major shift. In the early years of clinical legal education at Rutgers Law, the predominant model was for each clinic to be directed by a tenured or tenure-track faculty member and staffed by clinic staff attorneys employed under fixed-term contracts. The staff attorneys had no real job security and little status with the faculty. They were perceived to be skilled lawyers but not law faculty.

Over the years, things shifted, partly because of pressure from the ABA, legal education's accrediting agency, to give clinical instructors status and governance responsibilities comparable to "podium" faculty. At Rutgers Law, things came to a head first in 1990, when the denial of tenure to a faculty member who had assumed heavy clinical responsibilities triggered a broader debate about the status of clinical faculty and led to somewhat enhanced job security for clinical personnel and especially staff attorneys.

In the late 1990s, there was an even more intense second round when the faculty, after elaborate discussion (including a daylong retreat), agreed to create clinical professorships to replace clinic staff attorney positions.

Although neither a faculty vote nor tenure status were attached to the clinical professorships, they did elevate the positions by having them parallel tenured or tenure-track positions with two successive three-year terms, followed by five-year renewable terms. Successful candidates could move from assistant to associate to full clinical professor. In virtually all cases, however, the expanded job security of clinical faculty was conditioned on the availability of funding, and many of the positions were funded by "soft" money. Although clinical faculty members were not given voting rights, their "compensation" was they could serve on faculty committees.

In 2004, there was a much more expansive, and even more regrettably adversarial, debate focused on voting rights of clinical faculty. That had been a central part of the debate since at least 1990, but it resurfaced with a special vengeance. Because Rutgers Law had a relatively undersized tenured and tenure-track faculty and a relatively large clinical faculty, giving the latter substantial voting rights on institutional matters was perceived by some senior tenured faculty as a threat. There was concern that clinical faculty would vote as a bloc and, with the support of some tenured and tenure-track faculty, could control the school and possibly use that power to change the institutional mission and redirect Rutgers Law's relatively meager resources in ways that might be antithetical to the views and interests of some.

This triggered a broader, and at least equally heated, debate among tenured faculty about the law school's mission and priorities, with some senior faculty lining up in favor of the primacy of what they called "the scholarship of ideas" and others advocating a more pluralistic vision of how faculty should function. In a sense, this was a revisiting of the old tension between the law school as a university-based academic program or as a professional program whose primary mission was to prepare highly competent practicing attorneys. In more recent years, when variants of that debate have resurfaced, the competing visions have been rather uncharitably characterized in terms of the law school as "institute of advanced legal studies" or as "trade school."

Eventually, though, cooler heads prevailed, and a reasonable compromise emerged and was adopted regarding clinical faculty status, academic freedom and voting rights. The vehicle was the Clinical Scholar Series, under which existing clinical professors could opt to participate and all newly hired clinical professors were required to.

The *Rutgers Law School News* of April 2006 described the program in the following terms:

The Tumultuous Later Years (1978–2008)

The newly-developed series is designed to promote scholarship by clinical faculty, encourage their teaching of classroom courses, and provide them with a greater role in the governance of the law school.[97]

Completion of the clinical scholarship requirement—which can be accomplished through practice- or pedagogy-oriented writings directed to lawyers, judges and other clinical professors—would lead to "for cause" tenure-like job security for "hard money" clinicians and greater obligations by the school to retain "soft money" clinicians who complete the track.

Two clinical professors were appointed to the Clinical Scholar Series in 2006. Clearly, this initiative represented an effort to bridge the divide that had separated the clinical and "podium" faculty, albeit in an incremental manner. Clinical professors in the Clinical Scholars Series would be able to vote on all matters other than tenure-track personnel matters. In exchange, they would have to assume some scholarly duties and would be encouraged to assume some regular classroom teaching responsibilities. Unlike other clinical faculty, they also would be entitled to sabbatical leaves and other support for their research and writing.

The proverbial jury is still out on how successfully the Clinical Scholars Series is working. Part of the difficulty in evaluating it is that the past three years have been years of budgetary constraints, making the full funding of the program problematic. Still, conceptually, it represents a major step forward in the full integration of the clinical faculty into the broader law faculty, and it has eased most of the obvious institutional tensions that attended the process of reaching a decision.

Looked at from the perspective of the past thirty or more years, clinical faculty have traveled a long and complicated but productive road from staff attorney status to clinical professor status to clinical scholar status. Even that last status falls short of full parity with tenured and tenure-track faculty, but it represents an impressive closing of the gap.

The Rutgers Law clinical program has made impressive strides in another direction—the unification and coordination of the entire clinical program at the same time that the range of clinics has been diversified and expanded.

In the earlier years, the clinics were sometimes criticized as independent "fiefdoms" or as "ships passing in the night." This was partly a result of the configuration of 15 Washington Street, where individual clinics tended to be physically isolated.

Now, thanks to the magnificent clinical area, the isolation has ended. Even more important is the role Jon Dubin, a tenured faculty member, has played since 2002 as overall director of the clinical programs. With a deputy director, Bob Holmes, drawn from the clinical series faculty and an assistant director for administration, the way in which the clinics function has been revolutionized. In effect, we have a single coordinated program with the constituent clinics working to provide collaborative, coordinated and holistic representation of clients and the community. This has led to numerous instances in which clinics have collaborated in representing clients, to joint grants and other funding, to joint community legal education projects and workshops, to jointly taught classes and even to co-authored clinical scholarships across clinic lines.

The clinical program has also diversified in impressive ways. In the early years, there were three clinics, all heavily oriented toward litigation in the courts. The Urban Legal Clinic was the "small" case clinic; the Constitutional Litigation Clinic was the "big" case clinic; and the Women's Rights Litigation Clinic was the "specialized" case clinic. Each was headed by a tenured or tenure-track faculty member.

The Urban Legal Clinic (ULC) still has an emphasis on small case litigation, assisting low-income clients with legal problems that are caused or exacerbated by urban poverty. In a sense, since its founding in 1970, it has been the program most directly responsive to the late-1960s effort to get Rutgers Law to serve its local community. ULC has diversified its work over the years by engaging law students in community education, assisting volunteer lawyers in providing support and advice to family members of 9/11 victims, conducting legislative analyses and submitting comments on legislative bills affecting ULC's clients and providing law-related education workshops for children confined in the Essex County Juvenile Detention Center with an emphasis on juvenile justice matters that engage students in a range of legal work on behalf of children and young adults.

The Constitutional Litigation Clinic continues to function with great distinction primarily as a big case clinic, working on cutting-edge constitutional reform.

The four newer clinics dramatically diversify the offerings and experiences available to Rutgers Law students. The Community Law Clinic is Rutgers Law's only fully non-litigation clinic, focusing on transactional work. It also is one of the nation's first clinical programs to combine community development, corporate and real estate law and intellectual property law. As its official description puts it, "Students provide legal start-up services to public interest–oriented entrepreneurs and act as counsel to small businesses, non-profits, charter schools and major community development corporations in an effort to help transform blighted communities by creating employment opportunities, supportive local services and institutions, and affordable housing."

The Federal Tax Law Clinic engages students in all aspects of disputes between the Internal Revenue Service (IRS) and low-income taxpayers in New Jersey, including negotiations with the IRS and appearances in IRS administrative proceedings and before the tax court. Clinic students also help the American Friends Service Committee in its outreach to the immigrant community on tax matters.

The Child Advocacy Clinic serves the needs of children and their families who are at risk and living in poverty in Newark and surrounding areas. To advance that objective, clinic students engage in direct advocacy, representing children and their families in mediation conferences, administrative hearings and court proceedings. They also engage in community education and outreach and in policy and program development. Finally, the Child Advocacy Clinic, with the help of its students, serves as the law guardian for a number of abused, neglected and often disabled children who are residing in foster care.

The Special Education Clinic seeks to address the critical shortage of legal assistance for indigent parents of children with disabilities in New Jersey. Clinic students represent and advocate for parents and caregivers seeking an appropriate education for their children before school district child study teams, in mediation conferences and in proceedings before administrative law judges. Students also help to prepare materials for, and participate in, workshops offered by the clinic for family court judges, kinship givers, probation officers, law guardians, child welfare workers and parents, as well as for lawyers interested in developing the expertise to represent indigent parents and caregivers of children with disabilities.

A restructured Environmental Law Clinic plans to focus on environmental justice advocacy concerning pollution, hazardous sites and other environmental problems that directly affect communities and ecosystems in Newark and northern New Jersey. One issue that students working on the restructuring identified as an immediate concern was childhood lead poisoning.

Although Rutgers Law's clinical programs may not be as far ahead of the curve as they once were, they are still extremely impressive. In recent years, they have received a number of coveted awards reflecting their collective and individual excellence, including the 2009 Rutgers Chancellor's Community Engagement Award for the entire clinical program, the 2007

Clinical Legal Education Association's Clinical Case of the Year Award for the Constitutional Litigation Clinic's *Jama* case[98] and, several years earlier, CLEA's Top New/Emerging Clinician Award to Esther Canty-Barnes, director of the Special Education Clinic. Over the same time period, clinical faculty have assumed important positions with the AALS's Clinical Section, CLEA's board of trustees and the *Clinical Law Review*'s board of editors.

Today's clinics cover a far wider spectrum of subject matters and lawyering approaches and skills than the original clinics. In truth, they also seem to respond much more directly and substantially to the imperatives of the ABLS indictment of Rutgers Law in 1969 and the Tripartite Commission's response in 1970.

The Broader Curriculum

On the non-clinical curriculum front, there also were some significant shifts during the period between 1978 and 2008, but only one might reflect notable movement toward strengthening the commitments of the late 1960s and early 1970s—the enhancement of skills training.

The experiment of requiring Legal Representation of the Poor for first year students had ended by 1975. An examination of the school's curriculum in the ensuing years suggests that the Tripartite Commission's stated goal of allowing students to specialize in urban studies, or in a specific area of law, had limited success, and that was mainly through the clinics and interdisciplinary studies. While a number of courses and seminars dealing with civil rights and constitutional law issues continue to be offered—and there are opportunities to study other, more specialized areas of law relevant to the disenfranchised—these seem more dependent on the teaching and research interests of individual faculty members than on a sustained institutional commitment.

For most of the period between 1978 and 2008, the Rutgers Law curriculum has mirrored what many other law schools offer. That may be because, as a law school with a relatively small full-time tenured and tenure-track faculty, our ability to focus and enrich the curriculum in particular subject matter areas is limited. In fact, many of the distinctive and specialized courses and seminars are offered by adjunct faculty, mostly practicing attorneys or judges.

We still have a few distinctive curricular wrinkles that relate to, but hardly go to the heart of, the Tripartite Commission's transformative recommendations. Even through times of fiscal constraint and dwindling faculty teaching resources, we have maintained a "small section" policy under which every first-year student is assured that in one of the required courses he or she will be in a section of approximately thirty students, as well as an intensive first-year legal research and writing program.

Although the Tripartite Commission did make a recommendation regarding both legal writing and small sections, it had proposed that legal writing be taught by tenured or tenure-track faculty as part of a small section of a substantive course, thereby integrating it into the first-year curriculum. Such an approach was implemented for a time but was abandoned, partly at least, because of faculty opposition. Now, small sections largely present the same material in the same manner as larger sections, and legal research and writing functions independently of the rest of the first-year curriculum, taught by a separate cadre of instructors.

One limited first-year curricular innovation has been adopted independent of the Tripartite Commission's seminal work: an elective course focusing on legal or policy matters other than those derived from appellate court decisions and usually taught by means other than the so-called case method.[99] Although the first-year elective courses change from year to year, they can be grouped into three broad categories:

- Courses, such as Federal Income Tax and Professional Responsibility, designed to introduce students to the legislative process and to statutory (and regulatory) interpretation.
- Courses, such as Poverty Law, Education Law and Policy and Housing Policy, designed to provide students with the opportunity to study a public interest subject matter in an area of law that can be used primarily to represent the poor or disadvantaged.
- Courses, such as Fact Investigation and Alternative Dispute Regulation, designed to provide students with the opportunity to receive training in essential lawyering skills.

Most of these first-year electives are open to upper-level students, which creates a challenging but stimulating classroom dynamic as students ranging from 1L to 3L engage the same materials and participate in common discussions.

The last of the three categories of first-year electives—training in essential lawyering skills—requires some amplification. One of the Tripartite Commission recommendations was that Rutgers Law should do much more to train its students for the practice of law, a common refrain of legal education reformers for most of the past one hundred years. This is an area in which Rutgers Law quietly, almost surreptitiously, has made significant progress over the past thirty years. There are now a multiplicity of courses and seminars, as well as clinical experiences and moot court and mock trial competitions, focusing on a wide range of skills. They also reflect the diversification and globalization of law practice.

For example, to take just one lawyering skill, albeit an essential one—negotiations—there are courses and seminars in negotiations, adversarial negotiations, corporate negotiations, negotiating and implementing treaty regimes, negotiating and drafting entertainment contracts, negotiating and structuring complex corporate transactions and labor negotiations. The seminar component of a number of the clinical programs also deals with negotiation.

There is a similarly rich assortment of offerings in the area of trial practice and appellate advocacy, including a new and very intensive intersession course that involves law students, on a full-time basis for a week, interacting with and being mentored by seasoned attorneys and judges as they engage in a simulated trial. If this type of course succeeds, it is likely to be replicated in other skill areas. It could also be supplemented by distance or online interactive learning.

The heart of the upper-level curriculum itself has seen relatively limited changes over the thirty-year period covered by this chapter. Of course, a substantial number of courses and seminars have been introduced that reflect emerging, cutting-edge trends in the law, as well as faculty interests. These include elective courses in Advanced Intellectual Property; Business Torts and Intellectual Property; Electronic Commerce; Energy, Economics and the Environment; Global Climate Change: Science, Law and Economics; International Environmental Law; Internet Law; Islamic Jurisprudence; Law of Military Service and Armed Conflicts; National Security Law; Pharmaceutical Patent Law; and Political and Corporate Corruption Law, as well as seminars in the International Court of Justice, International Law and Terrorism, the Literature of Law and Markets and Science and International Law.

Looking at the curriculum as a whole through Rutgers Law's current master course list, one characteristic emerged strongly—the curriculum, as well as the faculty and students, is diverse and pluralistic. Based on an unscientific tally, with some admitted value judgments and double-counting, the curriculum shows remarkable balance among five different categories:

Table 1.

	General/ Core	Corporate/ Commercial	Public Interest/ Serving the Underserved	Skills	Cutting-Edge
Required	6	1	1	2	--
Elective courses	30	36	15	26	19
Seminars	6	8	22	5	8
Clinics	--	2	6	6	--
TOTAL	42	47	44	39	27

The faculty, directly and through its curriculum and policy committees, has periodically discussed sweeping curricular reforms, from fundamentally revamping the entire first-year curriculum to re-conceiving the upper years, especially the third, to creating concentration requirements. But the faculty has been unwilling to embrace any of those reforms, even when they were proposed by committees after substantial study and with detailed recommendations.

Part of the explanation for this resistance to fundamental curricular change may be the relatively small size of the tenured and tenure-track faculty (already mentioned and to be discussed in greater detail later in this chapter), but part may be a function of an irony or paradox. Despite Rutgers Law's well-deserved reputation as a progressive, even pioneering, law school, a substantial number of non-clinical faculty members are actually quite conservative in their approach to legal education and pedagogy. And others may simply be unwilling to change the established curricular order because it will require them to alter their teaching patterns and, perhaps, invest more time in teaching, leaving less for scholarly or other pursuits.

Whatever the precise combination of explanations, the paucity of curricular reform is clearly exacerbated by the existence of a separate part-time program. Reinstituted in 1975 by legislative mandate, the part-time program serves the positive purpose, consistent with Rutgers Law's historic commitment to expand opportunities, of enabling students who can't attend law school on a full-time basis due to family or job obligations to attend part-time and receive their degrees in about four years.

In restarting the program after a long hiatus, the faculty adopted two important policies: first, that the admissions standards for the full-time and part-time programs should be comparable so that students could freely transfer from one to the other; and second, that at least the required courses in the part-time program would be taught by regular tenured or tenure-track faculty. In addition, there have been efforts to make it feasible for part-time students to participate in a clinical experience, but that has proven to be difficult to implement.

The local folklore, and perhaps the truth, is that the law school was promised a number of additional faculty lines by the university because of the added burdens of having a part-time evening program and substantially more students. Several lines did seem to be added in the last half of the 1970s, and by the early 1980s Rutgers Law had forty-three tenured and tenure-track faculty members, its high-water mark. Since that time, by a process of erosion triggered by departures leaving unfilled lines and budgetary constraints that wound up with unfilled lines being stripped, the size of the faculty diminished to its current thirty-five. Teaching responsibilities and burdens have not been commensurately reduced, however.

Most faculty members who have taught in the part-time program have come to admire and respect the students and enjoy teaching them, but the program undeniably strains Rutgers Law's already thinly stretched teaching resources.

Informal Concentrations or Specializations

Despite the various limitations on Rutgers Law's ability to provide as rich and deep a curriculum as it would like, it is still possible for students to stitch together a substantial, if informal, concentration in some areas of law. By way of example, a student committed to public interest law or to serving historically underserved communities, both thrusts of the ABLS Indictment and Tripartite Commission, could combine a considerable variety of curricular and extracurricular opportunities.

On the curricular side, in addition to participating in one or more of the clinics, students could enroll in courses such as a new course in Poverty Law, for which students successfully petitioned the law school (a successor of sorts to the early 1970s first-year course in Legal Representation of the Poor[100]), and courses or seminars in Corporate Social Responsibility; Current Issues in Public Interest Law; Education Law and Policy; Elder Law; Housing Law and Policy; Immigration Policy; Race, Class and Metropolitan Equity; Jurisprudence: Human Rights and Animal Rights; Juvenile Justice; Political and Corporate Corruption; Race and the Law; Sexual Orientation and the Law; Social Security Law; and Special Education Law.

Internship and externship programs, as well as independent study projects (often developed jointly by students and faculty members) and research assistantships with faculty members engaged in public interest research or other projects, offer still more curricular outlets within Rutgers Law. Among the most popular credit-bearing externships with a public interest or public service dimension are those with state and federal judges, the New Jersey attorney general and the federal public defender; in immigration law with either the Office of District Counsel of the Federal Bureau of Citizenship and Immigration Services (formerly INS) or the Immigrants Rights Program of the American Friends Service Committee; and with the National Labor Relations Board.

Additionally, students can enroll in elective courses and seminars not directly related to public interest matters but that are taught by faculty members well known to incorporate aspects of the public interest into their course materials and teaching. To give one example of many, Professor Jon Dubin, director of Clinical Programs at Rutgers Law, teaches Administrative Law in a way that highlights substantive and procedural due process concerns of impoverished individuals.

Finally, law students can register and receive up to six law school credits for graduate courses in other units of the university. They can also go far beyond that in terms of interdisciplinary studies by enrolling in one of five formal joint-degrees programs, most of which have a public interest/public service dimension (e.g., the JD/MA in criminal justice, the JD/MCRP in city and regional planning, the JD/MSW in social work and the JD/MD in medicine). Finally, they can coordinate, on a case-by-case basis, a program of study with many of the more than one hundred graduate degree programs offered by Rutgers at the masters or doctoral level and have some of those credits apply toward the Rutgers Law JD.

Students interested in developing an informal public interest specialization can augment these sorts of curricular activities with a variety of extracurricular programs, detailed following, which include pro bono programs, specialized fellowships, loan repayment assistance, student journals and student organizations.

Extracurricular Innovations

Although non-clinical curricular innovations since 1978 have been relatively limited and, to a significant degree, peripheral to Rutgers

Law's historic mission and commitments, there have been a number of "extracurricular" innovations of greater scope and resonance. They include formal programs in study skills offered both generally to all full- and part-time first-year students and specifically to MSP students; a variety of programs oriented toward public interest and pro bono activities; several relatively new, or newly configured, student journals; and an assortment of new student organizations with ambitious outreach, community education and service programs.

The two main study skills programs are similar in purpose, but they take different forms and have existed for vastly different periods of time. In the fall of 2006, the law school created a continuing orientation program for all full- and part-time first-year students conducted by law school administrators. The program is designed to assist them in developing the study skills necessary for success in law school. It includes sessions on how to read a case, outline course material and prepare for and take final examinations. In connection with the last, the students take practice exams and are given individualized feedback.

Substantially earlier, Rutgers Law institutionalized "study skills" training for first-year MSP students. The current version of the program is organized around facilitated study groups and is known as the Legal Skills Study Group Program. While students at virtually all law schools in the country form and develop informal study groups, Rutgers Law is one of the few schools with a formalized study group program.

This program was developed in response to concerns expressed in the 1970s that Rutgers Law was admitting students through the MSP (when, unlike now, it was a separate admissions program) but was not supporting them adequately when they arrived, often with educational, economic or other disadvantages.

Currently, students who participate in the MSP are required to attend a weekly one-hour study group session for each required first-year substantive law course in which they are enrolled. Each study group consists of eight to ten students and is facilitated by an upper-class student.[101]

Another type of extracurricular development and innovation is the Eric R. Neisser Public Interest Program. This program facilitates public interest activities and projects in order to engage students in public interest educational opportunities and explore public interest career options.

One component of the Neisser Program encourages students to undertake public interest work during law school through an incentive plan. By completing thirty-five hours of pro bono legal public service in law school–

sponsored activities or external community-based activities, students receive a notation on their transcript and a certificate upon graduation. In 2007, Rutgers law students conceived of Pro Bono Day, on which law students coordinate and participate in daylong local volunteer projects.

The Neisser Program also supports two student-pioneered efforts, the Domestic Violence Advocacy Project (DVAP) and the Street Law Program. Under the supervision of a staff attorney, DVAP student volunteers receive training and then utilize their newly learned skills at the Essex County Superior Court to provide information, advocacy, assistance and referrals to domestic violence victims. The Street Law Program trains law students to educate high school students in Newark public schools and other members of the Newark community on legal issues pertaining to their lives.

These programs embody Rutgers Law's commitment to public interest and public service and provide an outlet for students to contribute to the community even if they are unable to enroll in clinics or choose not to.

In addition to volunteer public service opportunities supported by the Neisser Program, students planning to pursue careers in public interest or public service may apply for one of two fellowship programs. The Kinoy-Stavis Fellowship Program aims to honor Arthur Kinoy's legacy as a civil rights attorney. Students selected for the program receive a stipend, spend an entire year working in the Constitutional Litigation Clinic and have the opportunity to do a summer internship with the Center for Constitutional Rights. They also are entitled to receive reimbursement for attendance at a public interest conference.

Kinoy fellows also are actively engaged in strengthening Rutgers' public interest programs. They plan and help to staff the annual First Monday Event, which is celebrated by law schools nationwide. They also participate in regular discussions concerning public interest law and brainstorm approaches to promote public interest opportunities at Rutgers.

Rutgers Law's second fellowship program was created in memory of an alumna, Marsha Wenk, who devoted her career to public interest law. Students selected as Wenk fellows receive a stipend and commit to serving an internship with the ACLU of New Jersey for one semester. The Wenk fellows also work with the Kinoy fellows to promote public interest opportunities at Rutgers Law.

The Neisser Program also supports two programs aimed specifically at students who plan to pursue public interest careers. One program, the Public Interest Law Foundation (PILF), is a student-run organization whose purpose is to raise funds to subsidize students interested in doing public interest work over the summer. The stipends enable students to take unpaid internships with organizations committed to public service. Most of PILF's funds are raised at a well-attended annual dinner and auction, which is a highlight of Rutgers Law's social calendar.

A similar project is the Loan Repayment Assistance Program (LRAP). LRAP recently celebrated its ten-year anniversary of providing graduates in pursuit of public interest careers with assistance in relieving some of their law school and undergraduate debt burdens. Originally, LRAP was funded solely through a self-assessed student fee, but it later received a large contribution from an anonymous alumnus. The Rutgers LRAP program is unique in that it is one of the only national LRAP programs to grant awards to every graduate who applies. These programs show the interest that Rutgers Law students take not only in public interest careers for themselves but also in helping their classmates to take jobs that they might otherwise be unable to afford to accept.

Rutgers Law also demonstrates its commitment to public interest and public service through its support of the Eagleton Institute of Politics' graduate fellowship program, which includes law students. Eagleton fellows enhance their understanding of government, politics and public affairs through classroom discussions with fellow graduate and professional students, by attending events with prominent elected and appointed public officials and, most importantly, by being placed in internships with legislative and executive offices of the federal, state and municipal governments in New Jersey.

In recent years, the Eagleton fellowship program has enabled law students to work with the U.S. Equal Employment Opportunity Commission in Newark, Newark mayor Cory Booker's office and the Office of the Public Advocate (who, until recently, was Ronald Chen, an alumnus and now vice-dean of Rutgers Law).

The bottom line about the public interest/public service specialization example is that Rutgers Law still provides its students with rich opportunities. However, the school has chosen not to specify or require a concentration in public interest/public service (or any other field). Rather, its approach has been to rely on students to fashion their own concentrations out of a mix of regular and special curricular offerings, combined with a range of extracurricular activities.

Students can choose to do the same in a variety of other areas, including aspects of corporate and commercial law, criminal law, labor and employment law, intellectual property law and international law/globalization.

Responding to Broader Challenges to Legal Education and Particularly to Public Law Schools

During the past three decades, Rutgers Law has withstood the main challenges to its core mission, at least for the time being. However, it also has had to confront broader challenges to legal education and to public law schools that have surfaced with force since the early 1990s. Most of these broader challenges have not yet been dealt with adequately. They include:

- Diminishing public support for higher education, especially public higher education, and the need to rely ever more heavily on tuition revenue and entrepreneurial activities.
- The confounding and largely negative effects on most law schools of the *U.S. News & World Report* rankings.
- The periodic resurfacing of major proposals to reshape legal education to improve the development of key professional skills beyond those limited ones taught by the "case method."
- The impact of technology on the practice of law, and the need for legal education to take more effective account of that.
- The recent economic recession, dwindling job market and consequent plight of law students.

Diminishing Public Support

Between 1997 and 2008, public support for Rutgers University has declined from 34.5 percent of its total budget to about 18 percent. Even more dramatically, state support of Rutgers as a percentage of the state's total spending has gone from 2.15 percent in 1989 to 0.98 percent in 2008. By any measure, but especially in relationship to its wealth, New Jersey provides substantially less support for higher education and for its state university than most other states.

A major consequence is that an increasingly large share of Rutgers' revenue comes from student tuition and fees, from less than 22 percent in 1997 to more than 26 percent in 2008. Since 2005, student tuition and fees have exceeded state aid and by a significantly increasing percentage every year.

Rutgers, the state university of New Jersey, has ceased referring to itself as "state-supported" and instead speaks of its being "state-assisted." Because of the close fiscal relationship between the university and Rutgers Law, this has had a major trickle-down effect on the law school.

Based on annual data submitted by every law school to the American Bar Association, and disseminated in collated form by the ABA, Rutgers Law's situation, by every fiscal and educational measure, has deteriorated as compared to most public law schools and especially to its peer public law schools, such as Connecticut, Temple and Maryland. Even Pittsburgh and Penn State (formerly Dickinson), located in the general geographic area but not considered peers, have eclipsed Rutgers Law by those measures. Public law schools we have considered "aspirational," such as Illinois, Indiana, Ohio State and Iowa, are receding further into the distance by these benchmarks.

Resources and what they buy educationally have become an increasingly greater challenge for Rutgers Law, and in the final chapter there will be a discussion of the efforts launched by the school's new dean, John Farmer.

USNWR *Rankings*

Virtually no one in the law school world has defended *USNWR*'s rankings since they were issued in 1994. Predictably, though, the criticism by highly ranked schools is muted. Articles and blogs are legion about how many law schools have descended into outright deception and falsehood in "gaming the system." One of the grossest examples is a school that inflated its spending per student by including the fair market value of the free online services that Westlaw and Lexis provide to all law students in the country.[102]

To its credit, Rutgers Law has been scrupulous about not gaming the system. Those who know the school and what it stands for expect nothing less, but make no mistake about it, Rutgers Law has paid a ranking price for its honesty and integrity.

The costs and negative consequences of *USNWR*'s rankings go beyond the pressure to be downright dishonest or somewhat deceptive, however. A recent study by the U.S. General Accounting Office concluded that law school reactions to the rankings were the main driver of increasing student tuition, even weightier than the decline in public fiscal support.[103] Another recent study asserts that they have caused a decline in minority law students.[104]

The latter study highlights a particular stress point for Rutgers Law presented by the rankings: our historic commitment to student diversity and the MSP, substantially documented in this Centennial book. On average, black and Latino students, and educationally and economically disadvantaged white students, have lower LSAT scores than other white and Asian applicants. Since LSAT scores are a significant ranking factor, admitting applicants with higher LSAT scores, instead of those with lower scores, would tend to increase Rutgers Law's ranking just as it would inevitably diminish our diversity. Ironically, *USNWR* has a separate ranking of law schools by diversity, but diversity is not a positive factor in the general ranking. Indeed, for the reason described above, meaningful diversity actually has a depressing effect on the general ranking.

Another factor that tends to diminish a law school's ranking is spending relatively little to educate its students compared to other schools. One might think that educating students well for less is a positive accomplishment, although it's necessary to evaluate how you measure the quality of the education provided before you reach that conclusion. But *USNWR* seems to uncritically equate higher spending with better-quality education. Hence, there are stratagems, such as claiming you spend the fair market value of a free service. Because Rutgers Law spends substantially less than most other public law schools, that factor also hurts the ranking both directly and indirectly. Indirectly, it leads to a smaller faculty and higher student-faculty ratio, a ranking factor, and to less spending on the law library, another ranking factor.

Of course, the weightiest ranking factors are peer and lawyer-judge evaluations. Since most of us, including longtime legal academics, actually know very little about the ins and outs of more than a few law schools, what do you suppose most affects our impressions of all the other law schools? You guessed it—how highly they've been ranked. Isn't there some truism about self-fulfilling prophecies?

Proposals to Reshape Legal Education

At least once a decade for Rutgers Law's first one hundred years, a blue-ribbon commission has issued a report about the state of legal education and made recommendations to improve it. The reports, from earliest to latest, have said very similar things about legal education's preoccupation with an academic approach to educating future lawyers to the detriment of actually preparing them to practice law competently. The recommendations have ranged from Jerome Frank's rhetorical question "Why Not a Clinical Lawyering School?"[105] to proposed law school curricula developed around the core competencies required for law practice.

The two most recent major reports, along much the same lines as the earlier studies, were the 1992 *Report of the Task Force on Law Schools and the*

Profession: Narrowing the Gap (the "MacCrate Report")[106] and the 2007 report of the Carnegie Foundation for the Advancement of Teaching entitled *Educating Lawyers: Preparation for the Profession.*[107]

Both reports find that the interests of legal educators and the needs of legal practitioners are insufficiently connected for them to most effectively serve the public. They recommend a variety of ways in which the linkage can be strengthened and legal education should be substantially modified to reflect core professional skills and values in an integrated curriculum.

Although some law schools have taken these recommendations to heart and made fundamental changes in their approaches, most have not. Despite occasional rhetoric to the contrary, it is mostly business as usual in the legal academy.

With its early and heavy emphasis on clinical education, and its growing emphasis on professional skills training, Rutgers Law has been better positioned than many law schools to move in the recommended directions. Yet it has not done so in a systematic way, partly because of its undersized faculty and partly because of resistance from those who hold to the "academic" vision of legal education. Perhaps the recent economic recession and the need both to raise entrepreneurial funds and to "rebrand" itself may move Rutgers Law more substantially in that direction, but given the school's recent history of reform, it is unlikely to happen quickly and easily. Indeed, revisiting the history of Rutgers Law's rapid transformation in the late 1960s and early 1970s, makes one gasp in awe at the boldness and speed of the faculty's action.

The Impact of Technology

One of many important changes in the world of law practice, the world of higher education and the world generally is the impact of technology. Over recent years, more and more law firms have turned to technology to improve both the business and professional dimensions of their operations. More and more law students arrive at our doors having been educated and acculturated with heavy doses of technology.

Although Rutgers Law's current building, opened in 2000, was advertised as the most technologically advanced law school then—and it may still be among the leaders—it has had surprisingly little impact on the way faculty members teach and students learn, at least in the classroom. Few faculty members use the technology to do more than show an occasional video clip. That may be because old ways die hard, or it may be because, since law professors receive no training in teaching, they tend to teach their students the way they were taught. At the risk of beating a dead horse (with apologies to Gary Francione), an added reason at Rutgers Law may be its inadequate resources. With an undersized faculty and support staff, it is even more difficult to break out of an accustomed mold.

The days when legal education was dominated by a faculty member standing in front of a class and using a mixed lecture/"Socratic" dialogue approach have to be ending soon.[108] For law schools determined to hang on to that model, many believe that the market will bypass them. You can't serve a profession and attract a student body by providing a "product" that is increasingly disconnected from both markets, at least if you're not among the "elite" schools.

That's not to say that legal education should be a totally dehumanized, long-distance enterprise. Human interaction is important for good education and for the effective practice of law. It just has to be combined with the benefits of technology that is well conceived and well integrated into the educational process.

An Unholy Trinity: Economic Recession, Disappearing Legal Jobs and Hard-pressed Students

The last several years for Rutgers Law have been complicated on a number of levels by the economic downturn. State support for the university and the law school has continued to decline. Since most of our students have limited financial means, they are being pressed ever harder to make ends meet. And if those efforts, and accumulating indebtedness, are met with a scarcity of jobs, then the whole enterprise may be shaky. Even some of the elite law schools are expressing concern about whether there will be a continuing flow of students willing and able to spend tens of thousands of dollars per year when the pot of gold at the end of the proverbial rainbow may be seriously diminished.

For the moment, Rutgers Law may find this a standoff. Fewer students overall may be willing to take this gamble, but Rutgers Law's relatively low in-state tuition—barely half of the tuition at most private, and even some high-flying public, law schools—could maintain the applicant pool. We and other law schools may be hurt in another way, however. One of USNWR's ranking factors is the percentage of graduates employed immediately and within nine months. There's no telling how substantially the current recession may affect those percentages and how evenly the impact will be spread across law schools.

As the early chapters of this book indicate, this will hardly be the first serious challenge the economy and world events have posed for Rutgers Law. It has survived, although just barely a few times, two world wars, other wars hot and cold, the Great Depression and other fiscal reverses and urban upheavals in our own backyard.

Yet we have emerged from the first one hundred years a bit bloody but unbowed—in important ways, a stronger law school than we have been for much of our history. Our core commitments to diversity, public interest and public service and experiential learning, especially through clinical education, have survived difficult challenges. And so has our belief in a pluralistic law school and faculty with many accepted models to satisfy the university's three principal criteria—teaching; research and scholarship; and service.

Rutgers Law's next one hundred years will undoubtedly present as many challenges as the first hundred—some already identified immediately above, others seeking to catch us by surprise. Our success at meeting them all will be the subject of another chronicler, but the final chapter, an epilogue of sorts, will look briefly ahead. Before that, though, this chapter will conclude with a brief snapshot of Rutgers Law in 2008–9, the bridge between our first and next one hundred years, and the following chapter will conclude the Centennial history with the voices and visions of administrators and faculty, many larger than life, and of students in the Centennial Seminar who inspired this book.

A Snapshot of Rutgers Law as We Celebrate the Centennial[109]

Student Body. There are 575 full-time day students and 240 part-time evening students. The 191 day and 69 evening students in the 2009 entering class were selected from 3,510 applicants and come from 19 states, 25 countries and 137 undergraduate institutions. About 39 percent of the entering class and 37 percent of the total student body are students of color, and 43 percent of both are women.

Faculty. There are a total of fifty-nine tenured or tenure-track, clinical, library and legal research and writing (LRW) faculty. Of that total, thirty-five are tenured or tenure-track, ten are clinical, seven are library and seven are LRW. More than 43 percent are women, and almost 29 percent are people of color. In addition, there are ninety-one adjunct faculty members from bench, bar and the public and private sectors.

The Center for Law and Justice—a view from the courtyard in front of the school's current building.

Law Library. Although the library has been severely underfunded in recent years, at more than 558,000 volumes and volume equivalents it is still the largest law library in New Jersey. It also houses the School of Criminal Justice's collection, one of the leading collections in the world.

Clinical Program. There are six functioning clinics—Constitutional Litigation, Community Law, Child Advocacy, Federal Tax Law, Special Education Law and Urban Legal—and the Environmental Law Clinic is being restructured. More than 60 percent of all students take at least one live-client clinic before they graduate.

Other Programs. The Eric Neisser Public Interest Program, the Domestic Violence Advocacy Project, the Street Law Program, the Global Legal Studies Program and Study Abroad at Leiden University are programs of Rutgers Law. Programs outside the law school in which law students regularly participate are the Institute on Education Law and Policy and the Division of Global Affairs.

Externships. Rutgers Law students regularly participate, usually for academic credit, in a variety of externships, including those with federal and state court judges, the federal public defender, the National Labor Relations Board and the New Jersey attorney general. There are also externships in immigration law and intellectual property.

Student Journals. Students publish five journals, several of which were path-breaking. They include *Rutgers Law Review, Rutgers Computer and Technology Law Journal, Women's Rights Law Reporter* (first legal periodical in the United States focusing exclusively on the field of women's rights law), *Rutgers Race and the Law Review* (second legal journal in the United States focusing on the broad spectrum of multicultural issues) and *Rutgers Law Record* (first general interest fully online law journal).

Interdisciplinary Studies. The following joint degrees are available pursuant to structured programs: JD/MA in political science or criminal justice; JD/MBA in management or accounting; JD/MCRP in urban planning; JD/MD in medicine; and JD/MSW in social work.

Job Placement. For the class of 2007, the most recent graduating class with relatively complete data, 96 percent of the graduates were employed, and the breakdown of types of positions was as follows: private practice—46 percent; judicial clerkships—25 percent; business/industry—15 percent; government—5.5 percent; public interest—4.5 percent; academic—3 percent; and military—0.5 percent.

Alumni. There are more than 10,200 living alumni in virtually every state and in nineteen other countries out of a total alumni body of almost 12,500 for whom there are records. During most of Rutgers Law's early years, the graduating classes were relatively small, so the total number of deceased alumni is substantially less than the total number of living alumni. For a list of prominent alumni, see Appendix VI.

As with all snapshots, this one captures only a limited slice of Rutgers Law's complicated status and historical reality. Chapter 7, an epilogue of sorts, will use a relatively brief yet more textured and focused picture of the present as a springboard to the future and will hazard some predictions of what the next one hundred years might hold in store.

CHAPTER 6

THE VOICES AND VISIONS OF RUTGERS LAW

Concluding the Centennial History

A book about Rutgers Law would not be complete without two things: a remembrance of both some of the most colorful characters who populated the law school during its first one hundred years and some of their most memorable contributions to the school's mythology, and the voices of some recent students who had the idea of producing this book, students from the Centennial Seminar of 2008–9.

OF CHARACTERS AND CONTRIBUTIONS

In its first one hundred years, Rutgers Law undoubtedly has had at least that number of memorable or important characters. As with so much of this book, though, this chapter will have to be highly selective. And to a large extent, that selectivity will be framed by Professor Tractenberg's personal experience here over the past four decades, as well as the events and characters with whom he's had contact.

The early years of the school resonate with some important and fascinating personalities, however, and they have to be included. Many have already been at least mentioned in historical context but not discussed in detail.

The first of those is Richard Currier, the founder of New Jersey Law School in 1908. Consider the vision, imagination and energy—and perhaps the presumptuousness—of someone only a few years beyond his own law school education who decided to launch New Jersey's first law school.

What we know about Currier suggests that he was a vigorous and effective educational entrepreneur. New Jersey Law was for decades a for-profit

A crowd of students, staff and faculty in the atrium at an event. *Courtesy of Shelley Kusnetz.*

proprietary law school, a widely employed model then. After it survived the challenges of a start-up process, increasing regulation and escalating standards by the responsible state and professional authorities and a world war, by the mid-1920s New Jersey Law had well over 2,300 students enrolled, making it the largest or second-largest law school in the nation. That strongly suggests that Currier's entrepreneurial efforts were well-rewarded, and he sought to maintain his control over the law school as it went through a series of transformations.

Currier's commitments went beyond the entrepreneurial, though. From the start, he was committed to opening New Jersey Law's doors to nontraditional law students—those who had to work to earn their tuitions, those who had recently arrived in the United States and in New Jersey and those who by their gender tended to be ignored or excluded from legal education. Currier wrote in 1901 that "[e]ducation may not be the panacea of every social evil [but it is] a most potent factor in the progress of human development toward the ideal in the individual and the state."[110]

One of the women who benefited from Currier's vision was Elizabeth Blume Silverstein, who graduated from New Jersey Law in 1911 as a member of the school's second graduating class but not the first female graduate.

Elizabeth Blume, as she was known then, had wanted to be a lawyer from a young age. When she was a high school student, one of her teachers asked the class what each wanted to be. Elizabeth responded that she wanted to be a lawyer. The teacher pulled her aside and urged her to pick a profession suitable for women. Being a quick learner, Elizabeth "recanted" and told her classmates that she wanted to be a nurse.

When the opportunity to pursue a legal education at New Jersey Law materialized, however, Elizabeth seized it. Since she was too young to be admitted to the bar when she graduated in 1911, Elizabeth tried to find a job with a lawyer, but she was repeatedly rebuffed. Finally, when she came of age and was admitted in 1913, Elizabeth hung out her shingle. She remained active in the private practice of law for more than seventy years and was the first woman in New Jersey to represent a defendant in a murder case on her own.

In October 1935, New Jersey Law and its Newark-based competitor, Mercer Beasley Law School, were combined and became the law school of the new University of Newark, under the presidency of Frank Kingdon. By all accounts, Kingdon was a larger-than-life character. He also clearly, like

Dr. Frank Kingdon, president of the University of Newark.

Currier, was in the progressive tradition of the time. His strongly articulated view was that the University of Newark had both to provide opportunities to the widest student population and engage the broader community.

As to the education of women, Kingdon seemed very much to agree with Currier. In a 1940 biography Kingdon wrote about the legendary John Cotton Dana, founder of the Newark Museum and the second librarian of the Newark Public Library, Kingdon highlighted a quote he found in Dana's papers:

> *Every woman should be trained for a job. Every woman who knows enough to do it should take advantage of every possible opportunity to promote the independence of women. No young woman should be expected to stay at home or take care of her parents with any greater degree of expectancy than is extended to the young men of the family.*[111]

Given his social credo and his background as a prominent member of the clergy, it is hardly a surprise that Kingdon quickly became embroiled in controversy. Unfortunately for the new university and for Kingdon's tenure as its president, the controversy erupted just as he was launching a major capital campaign in April 1938. In rapid-fire succession, Kingdon took on three major forces in New Jersey: the local Catholic leadership, the German-American community and the storied Jersey City mayor, Frank Hague.

In response to an attack by a Catholic cleric, Father Matthew Toohey of St. James Church, on the University of Newark and its faculty as "communistic" and "honeycombed with radicals of the most extreme type," Kingdon said that "[t]he University of Newark is exactly as radical as the constitution of the United States, which guarantees the freedom of speech to all its citizens."[112] This incident was a precursor, but sharp contrast, to the disgraceful behavior of the university in the mid-1950s, when it jettisoned several faculty members, including Professor Abraham Glasser of the law school, during the communist witch hunts of that era.

Kingdon also alienated many members of the German-American community with his sharp denunciations of Nazis—in Germany and in Newark. And he completed the trifecta by taking on the powerful Mayor Hague. In the last effort, Kingdon was joined by Spaulding Frazier, who was the pre-merger dean of Mercer Beasley and then the dean of the merged University of Newark law school. Frazier joined attorneys for the CIO and the still young ACLU "to oppose forcible removal of CIO organizers from Jersey City"[113] on Hague's orders. This prompted Father Toohey to defend Hague in the following apocalyptic terms:

The battle of the century is being fought in Jersey City to determine whether the brand of Americanism that we know is to prevail or whether the brand of Americanism that is endeavored to be proclaimed by Morris Ernst and Roger Baldwin [a founder of the ACLU] *and his ilk will prevail.*[114]

Hague weighed in with his own overheated rhetoric:

We hear about constitutional rights, free speech and free press. But every time I hear these words, I say to myself "that man is a Red, that man is a Communist."[115]

The case of *Hague v. CIO* reached the U.S. Supreme Court and resulted in a landmark decision affirming the CIO's First Amendment right of free association.[116] Still, pressure from Toohey and Hague led to Kingdon's apparently forced resignation from the presidency of the University of Newark.

The law school's next (and current) incarnation as Rutgers School of Law–Newark came in 1946 when the entire University of Newark was absorbed by Rutgers, newly the state university of New Jersey. Since then, there has been no shortage of important, lively and even quirky characters. The array presented here is highly selective and highly personal to the faculty author of this Centennial history.

Lehan Tunks served as the school's dean from 1953 to 1962, during a period to which Professors George Thomas and Gary Francione referred in their published reminiscence as the first golden age of Rutgers Law.[117] It was a time when some faculty members wanted to fashion Rutgers Law into a public Yale law school. Tunks, with his Yale doctorate in "judicial science," seemed the perfect dean for that effort, and in part he was. Still, in a published tribute to him, Rutgers Law professor Allan Axelrod characterizes the kind of law school Tunks wanted as "a mixture of tough useful professional training and thoughtful scholarship that is legal education at its best."[118] That sounds more like a pluralistic vision, especially appropriate to a relatively newly minted state law school, than a "public Yale law school."

According to the Axelrod tribute, Tunks's charge was "to build a major state law school." To do so involved a number of ambitious and controversial reforms:

He had to position the school as a high priority claimant upon university resources: to effect large increases in library collection and staff, to break his faculty's salaries free from the university pattern, to acquire research and administrative resources, all of which generated disputes within the university. He led the faculty to decisions that entangled the newly visible public institution in external fights with bar, alumni, or the legislature. There was one year in which Newark admissions standards were so boosted as to cut the entering class by almost 50%, and there was a several-year campaign to drop the school's evening division as beyond its resources.[119]

This sounds eerily similar to the charge of Rutgers Law's current dean, John Farmer. In Axelrod's view, Tunks achieved a number, but not all, of his goals for Rutgers Law, and he did it "more by example than by precept."[120] One of his strengths in dealing with external and internal controversies was a "dazzling command of language" and "a quick wit." Tunks could "slice off an arm" with words or "dispel tension through his sense of humor, which could warm you for a week."[121] Axelrod, a master of words himself, was in awe of Tunks's "verbal mastery [that] enabled him to indulge a bizarre taste for baroque bureaucratese, so that our school did not have exams but 'accountability exercises,' and discussions of the length of classes and semesters dealt with 'time containers.' It was odd that he relished that kind of language; it was incredible that he could get others to use it."[122]

Willard Heckel was Rutgers Law's next dean, from 1963 to 1970, and again was acting dean from 1973 to 1974. He was different from Lehan Tunks in a number of important ways. For one, he was a local guy born, bred and educated—a product of New Jersey Law, class of 1940. He lacked a Yale pedigree, but he more than made up for that with street smarts, patently obvious decency and integrity and an extraordinary commitment to Rutgers Law and to the broader community.

With his partner, Malcolm Talbott, Willard Heckel led Rutgers Law through the controversy and wreckage of 1967 to the promised land of its second golden age—the era of fundamental transformation during which the MSP and clinical education programs were established and the commitment to using law to achieve social justice became a hallmark. And the "promised land" terminology was not just rhetorical; Willard Heckel was deeply religious, rising to become national moderator of the Presbyterian Church. For many reasons, he earned the respect of his faculty, the student body and the broader community in a tumultuous time. The fact that he and Malcolm Talbott were "perfect together," long before Governor Thomas Kean's administration coined that as a tourism phrase for New Jersey, added to Willard Heckel's mystique.

Malcolm Talbott.

In his own right, Malcolm Talbott was a major figure at Rutgers Law and in the broader community. A longtime law professor and associate dean, he served as a Rutgers vice-president from 1963 to 1974 with responsibility for the Newark campus. He preceded Provost Norman Samuels and current chancellor, Steven Diner, in that capacity. Talbott is generally credited with launching the modern development of the Newark campus. Appropriately, the first residence hall symbolizing Rutgers–Newark's shift from a purely commuter campus bears his name. After his vice-presidency, Talbott became president of the Rutgers Foundation.

In the period following the 1967 riots, Talbott pushed both for greater university involvement in the Newark community and for inter-institutional cooperation. He was a dominant figure in forming the urban university center now known as University Heights, a center that includes Rutgers, New Jersey Institute of Technology, Essex County College and the University of Medicine and Dentistry of New Jersey.

During that difficult and contentious time, Talbott earned the respect of the undergraduate Black Organization of Students and hosted many of the members at the commodious Mount Prospect Avenue apartment that he shared with Willard Heckel to the end of his life. He also was instrumental in working out a resolution of their grievances. Vickie Donaldson, the BOS spokesperson, maintained a friendship with Talbott until he died.

Talbott also earned the respect, admiration and fondness of his colleagues. A story is told about a time when there was a move afoot in the central Rutgers administration in New Brunswick to remove Talbott as vice-president in charge of the Newark campus, reportedly because he advocated so strongly on behalf of Newark that he wasn't a "team player." One of those who worked for him, a black woman named Delora Jones, asked her friends to support Talbott. According to a column published in the *Star-Ledger* about Delora after her death, "This was strange. Talbott was a Midwest WASP, who looked like a Prussian general and spoke like an Oxford don. Yet Delora knew he was good for Newark. Besides, he was her friend."[123]

Peter Simmons was another transplant from the Midwest by way of Ohio State Law School, although the West Coast and University of California–Berkeley may be closer to his heart. He became dean in 1975, after Jim Paul's relatively short deanship and Willard Heckel's and Al Blumrosen's one-year acting deanships, and remained in that position for eighteen years, the longest tenure of any Rutgers Law dean.

The Simmons deanship, like Rutgers Law itself, had its ups and downs. According to Gary Francione and George Thomas, it included Rutgers Law's third golden age beginning in 1984 (and continuing until 1995), when a substantial number of very bright and accomplished young faculty members were attracted to the school, and hopes were rekindled for Rutgers Law to vault into the top ten public law schools in the country.[124] This hope was aided and abetted by relatively strong economic times, which enabled Rutgers Law to increase the size of its faculty and the status of its library, among other institutional improvements. Peter Simmons had his strong supporters on the faculty, none more loyal and committed than John Payne and Diana Sclar, who alternated as associate deans for most of Simmons's long deanship.

However, the Simmons deanship also had more than its share of tough sledding. Partly, it was the sometimes bemused, and sometimes annoyed, reactions of faculty members to his personal quirkiness. For example, Simmons regularly arrived at the law school before some faculty members called it a night, and they would sometimes find "love" notes awaiting them in their offices, perhaps reminding them that they weren't permitted to tape things to their office walls.

A bigger problem developed in the early 1990s, however, and was related to Arthur Kinoy's mandatory retirement. Under federal law in effect then, most employees, including university faculty, were required to retire at age seventy, but Rutgers' policy permitted faculty members to remain beyond that age if they were determined to be "essential" to the particular school. Kinoy wanted to stay on, and many students and faculty colleagues were all for that. However, after a faculty debate and a closely divided vote on whether Kinoy satisfied the criteria for an exception, Simmons refused to request an exception for him, justifying it on the grounds of insufficient fiscal resources. That led to a confrontation with the faculty, ultimately about the lack of transparency of the law school's budgetary processes, and also Simmons's resignation from the deanship. He has remained in the law school as a university professor ever since.

A personal reflection Simmons prepared for this book concluded with the following guardedly optimistic paragraph:

> *We can deservedly be proud of the accomplishments of Rutgers Law's first 100 years—especially our contribution to diversifying the New Jersey bar—and at the same time, recognize our unrealized potential. With a new dean at the helm, and many gifted and energetic recently hired faculty, there is every reason to anticipate a new birth of creativity—if only we can overcome the persistent and crippling budget crises, which have been a constant feature of our institutional life over the past 35 years.*

To complete the picture of Rutgers Law's modern deans, Peter Simmons was followed in 1993 by Roger Abrams, who served a five-year deanship. Abrams came here to lead the effort to get a new law building funded and constructed, and he did that with aplomb. At Nova in his prior deanship, he had done the same. Indeed, during the faculty's "due diligence" inquiries about Abrams, one of his Nova colleagues, when pressed hard for something negative about him, said that other Nova deans were resentful of the magnificence of the new law building he had engineered there and had taken to calling it the "Rog Mahal."

Abrams was a consummate salesman and an incurable optimist. His glass was always half full. That extremely well-developed sense of optimism almost certainly led to his departure from Rutgers Law. In connection with what Abrams considered the university's botching of a very large gift for the

Dean Stuart Deutsch at a Centennial event.
Courtesy of Shelley Kusnetz.

new law building, he decided to take on Rutgers president Fran Lawrence *mano a mano*.

That led to a one-year acting deanship by Eric Neisser and the arrival of Stuart Deutsch in 1999 for a ten-year deanship. Deutsch actually presided over the completion and opening of the new law building in 2000. That was one of the high-water marks of another complicated deanship, which survived the longstanding controversy over the status of clinical faculty in relatively good shape. In recent years, as the state, the university and Rutgers Law lurched from one budgetary crisis to the next, Deutsch had to preside over successive shortfalls and ensuing retrenchments. Those don't make for especially enjoyable deanships, and yet the ship stayed afloat as the helm was turned over to Dean John Farmer.

In Rutgers Law's first one hundred years, it wasn't just law school and university administrators who were important, charismatic and colorful figures, though. During the 1960s, 1970s and beyond, there was a wide spectrum of faculty members who qualified, albeit for an impressive variety of reasons.

One dimension was scholarly and academic. In September 1966, to celebrate the opening of the then new Rutgers Law building—Ackerson Hall—Professors Julius Cohen and David Haber designed and administered a remarkable two-day, three-session symposium on the theme of "The Projection of an Ideal: The Law School of Tomorrow."[125] Each of the sessions dealt with a different aspect of legal education: Law as a Phase of the Humanities and as a Subject of the Behavioral Sciences; Directions for Research, Empirical and Nonempirical; and The Training of the

Practitioner. Yet again, the inevitably pluralistic nature of legal education at Rutgers Law emerged.

Each of the three seminar sessions was introduced by a distinguished senior member of the Rutgers Law faculty: Julius Cohen, Tom Cowan and Victor Brudney. Each session had an illustrious presenter, two distinguished commentators and nine or ten outstanding discussants. Together they represented a remarkable who's who of bench, bar and legal academy.

David Haber definitely qualifies as a notable faculty member for reasons other than his involvement with the 1966 symposium and follow-up book. He had an impressive educational and legal pedigree—from City College of New York to an LLB and law journal editorship at Yale Law School and then on to distinguished clerkships with Judge Charles Clark on the Second Circuit and Justice Hugo Black on the U.S. Supreme Court. While on the Yale Law School faculty in 1952, Haber co-authored with a senior colleague, Tom Emerson, what was probably the first casebook to deal comprehensively with emerging legal doctrines of civil rights.[126]

Despite these "leftist" credentials, Haber had more conservative— some called them elitist—impulses about internal institutional issues at Rutgers Law. They emerged periodically during heated faculty debates about student credentials and such. Perhaps because of his acting background and proclivities, Haber became well-known among his colleagues for the quivering voice and hand that signified especially deep feelings about those issues.

During his law school tenure and since, Haber has manifested other literary and artistic traits. He helped his colleague, Professor J. Allen Smith, found the Law & Humanities Institute in 1978, serving as its first chair. Haber is still an emeritus member of the institute's board of governors, and his Rutgers Law colleague, Saul Mendlovitz, a longtime teacher of law and humanities, serves on the distinguished advisory board. Thus, Rutgers Law's connection with that institute is deep, wide and ongoing.

Saul Mendlovitz is another man of many parts. In his fifty-fourth year on the Rutgers Law faculty, albeit now as a professor emeritus, he still teaches an engaging Law and Humanities seminar to a roomful of eager students. Over the years, he has co-taught the seminar with a variety of colleagues, including Haber, Smith and George Thomas. This year, he's working on a new recruit—Dean John Farmer Ironically, unlike many retirees, Mendlovitz is around the law school far more often now than he was during his full-time faculty days. In those years, he was jetting around the world, teaching every other semester at Columbia Law School or directing a project he founded in New York City, the World Orders Model Project. For more than half a century, Saul Mendlovitz has been one of the world's most articulate, persistent and respected voices speaking out against war, genocide and other forms of armed violence. It is no surprise that Rutgers Law had a required first-year course in International Law and a Just World Order, Mendlovitz's signature course. It also is no surprise that he largely inspired a field of study in world order at law schools across the country and world.

Mendlovitz has been a fixture at the lunch table in the faculty lounge for decades, raising provocative but civil questions of all his colleagues on a vast array of subjects. He and his dear friend and longtime colleague Allan Axelrod were worth the price of admission when they held court there. Colleagues who participated in or observed the wide-ranging discussions were often divided over who of the two was smarter or more widely read.

Mendlovitz also has been known to savor the fruit of the vine and become even more voluble and even less inhibited. In that he's had good company at Rutgers Law over the years. There was a time in the 1970s when some suspected that the faculty could have applied for its own AA chapter. The suspicion extended to the contents of the coffee cups some faculty members routinely took to class with them. Just because it was brown didn't necessarily mean it was coffee or tea, and just because it was colorless didn't necessarily mean it was water. It made for some really interesting classes.

J. Allen Smith, famed both for his law and literature accomplishments, as well as his southern gentleman's prowess with bourbon and branch water, managed to combine the two by quoting verbatim and at length from *Finnegan's Wake* when he was feeling no pain.

There were other eccentricities, too, that led to interesting classes. Gerry Moran was famous for the length, complexity and grammatical perfection of sentences he regularly spun out in his classes. Students used to transcribe his longer sentences to see if they could catch him in a grammatical error; rumor has it that they never did. At one class in the dead of winter, Moran was in rare form, uttering one super-length, multi-clause sentence after another. As he took a breath, he noticed a hand raised in the back of the large classroom. He hurriedly said, "Okay, I see you, just a second" and then continued his sentence. This happened several times, each time provoking louder snickers from the students. Finally, the class ended, and Moran realized that he'd never recognized the student who'd had his hand up for much of the class. He went to the back of the room to apologize and found, to the delight of his students, that he'd been dialoguing with a coat hanging on a hook.

Alan Schwarz was another superb, but decidedly eccentric, law teacher. His students loved him, and he engaged them actively and loudly. Schwarz was notorious for dressing like a derelict, although he was brilliant, erudite and sophisticated. He also smoked like a chimney, often in places at the law school where it wasn't permitted.

One year, not long after faculty author Tractenberg arrived at Rutgers Law, he had the dubious pleasure of teaching next door to Schwarz. His class occupied one section of the largest classroom in Ackerson Hall that could be partitioned into three by sliding wooden dividers with absolutely no soundproofing capacity. Schwarz's class was in the adjoining one. Frequently, Tractenberg had to pound on the dividing wall when Schwarz's class got so loud that neither Tractenberg nor his students could hear themselves think.

One day, Schwarz's class reached unprecedented decibel levels, and pounding on the partition had no effect. Tractenberg finally decided to use the connecting door in the partition and make his pleas for quiet more directly. He was stunned by what he saw: Schwarz was in a billowing cloud of smoke, surrounded by his students. They were frantically trying to put out the fire he had started in his sport jacket pocket when he put a still glowing cigarette there, apparently thinking that it was the chalk he always carried with him.

Cigarettes figure prominently in another classic Schwarz story, as does his widely noted lack of sartorial splendor. One evening, he went to a grocery store in Montclair, where he lived, to buy some cigarettes. He was dressed in his usual frayed herring bone gray jacket, with several days' growth and uncombed hair. As Professors Francione and Thomas recounted the story in their article:

> *This disheveled man picked up a pack of cigarettes and, being too impatient to wait in line, put a dollar close to the cash register and walked out the door. The clerk, not seeing the dollar, called the store manager, who accosted Schwarz[127] in the parking lot. He explained what had happened, they returned to the store, and the clerk told the manager that she had found the dollar. Schwarz demanded an apology from the manager, who refused to apologize. As Schwarz left the store, a police officer arrived and engaged him in conversation about the incident. At some point, the officer asked Schwarz for identification. Schwarz refused, saying that he was a professor of constitutional law and, therefore, knew that the officer had no right to compel him to identify himself. The conversation turned angry and the officer arrested Schwarz as a disorderly person.[128]*

In the police car, when Schwarz told the officer that he lived in Montclair, the officer was prepared to release him if Schwarz would provide his driver's license. Predictably, "Schwarz refused, standing on his constitutional rights."[129]

That wasn't the last of the "constitutional rights" assertions, though. At Schwarz's trial before a municipal court judge, he was represented by Rutgers Law colleague Norman Cantor, another constitutional law teacher. One version of the story of the trial, perhaps apocryphal, is that Cantor kept trying to assert the violation of Schwarz's constitutional rights, but the judge kept cutting him off to remind him that he was in municipal court. Finally, the judge told Cantor sternly that if the word "constitution" passed Cantor's lips once more he would hold him in contempt of court.

The bottom line is that Schwarz was found guilty and fined fifty dollars, and the case went down in the legal annals as the "Case of the Montclair One."[130]

Smoking figures prominently in yet another classic Rutgers Law story, this one involving Alex Brooks. Alex had his talents and accomplishments, but they tended to be diminished by his need to remind everyone that he was too good to be at Rutgers Law—the place he spent virtually his entire career. The annual alumni dinner used to feature faculty members who were retiring. It's hard to forget the one when Brooks, Schwarz and Axelrod were

Dean James Paul.

the honorees. Schwarz and Axelrod made witty, graceful presentations, and the assembled alums ate it up. Brooks basically said, to stony silence, that he was really glad to be retiring so that he could devote his time to important scholarly activities instead of having to spend a lot of it trying to teach dreary students. One has to acknowledge his chutzpah (for those unfamiliar with the word, it is legal Latin).

Given that introduction, the smoking story won't come as a shock. Brooks arrived at a tenured faculty promotion and tenure meeting in the elegant Provost's Conference Room of 15 Washington Street. He entered the room, sniffed the air and announced to all assembled that he smelled smoke, that this was a nonsmoking room and that he would leave the meeting unless anyone smoking ceased doing so. At that point, practically everyone in attendance, including a number of nonsmokers, lit up and began puffing away.

It's probably beginning to sound as if the Rutgers Law faculty of the 1970s could have used some enforcers, and it just so happens that there were a few who routinely terrorized students and sometimes terrorized their colleagues. Three come easily to mind. They were diverse, but each packed a wallop delivered by demeanor and force of personality.

Bob Knowlton, referred to as "Bullet Bob" as a sign of respect but also intimidation, was a big gruff-appearing bear of a man who many found actually had the proverbial heart of gold. Bullet Bob was a leading criminal law scholar and policy advocate beginning in the 1950s when he joined the Rutgers Law faculty. He was a co-author with Professor Sam Dash of Georgetown Law Center of a 1959 book entitled *The Eavesdroppers*, which many believed led to the reshaping of the nation's wiretapping laws. Dash, of course, was best known for his work as chief counsel to the Senate Watergate Committee and for his resignation in protest from the position of ethics adviser to independent prosecutor Kenneth Starr during the Whitewater Investigation when he felt that Starr exceeded his legal role as an objective investigator.

Then there was Eva Morreale Hanks, the first woman to join the faculty, the first to be tenured at Rutgers Law and a colleague between 1963 and 1972 of the second—Ruth Bader Ginsburg. If Malcolm Talbott was a midwestern WASP who looked like a Prussian general, Hanks was a Prussian (or at least a German) who *acted* like a Prussian general. Her slender blonde attractiveness masked the toughness underneath—at least for a time. Pity the faculty colleague who crossed her on a matter of internal politics or the student who didn't measure up in her class. Though Eva Morreale when she arrived at Rutgers Law, she became Eva Hanks after she married a former student, John Hanks. The marriage prompted a comment in the yearbook that many students always felt she favored law review students and that now she had proven it by marrying one.

Hanks left Rutgers Law in the mid-1970s, at least partly because her colleagues had not embraced the faculty aspirations of her husband with sufficient ardor. She joined the brand-new Cardozo Law School faculty as a founding member and remains there.

The third faculty enforcer was Al Slocum. Slocum was and is smart, committed, savvy and tough. His record of accomplishment amply demonstrates that. He played a truly seminal role as student leader and new faculty member in transforming Rutgers Law in the late 1960s and early 1970s, and he was a formidable advocate for the MSP whenever it came under attack.

Generations of Rutgers Law students can attest to all those qualities but perhaps mostly to his toughness, which became legendary. Slocum took "tough love" to a whole new level when it came to his classes. His rule was that students could not attend unless they were prepared. And he would test that often by grilling one student for the entire hour. Professors Francione and Thomas tell the story of a student in one of Slocum's classes who, when called on, said that he passed his turn:

> *Slocum told the student that he was not allowed to pass in a Slocum class. The student responded with a touch of defiance, that he had to pass because he was unprepared. Slocum then reminded the student of his rule that students were not allowed to attend class unless they were prepared. "You knew this was my rule?" "Yes." "You are present in class?" "Yes." "Then you must be prepared. Let me tell you the facts of the case and then you can answer my question." "No," the student said, "I am not prepared."*
>
> *Slocum looked at the student for a few seconds. The silence in the classroom was thick. Finally, he said, "I won't teach students who don't follow the rules." He closed his book and began to walk toward the door. "Class is dismissed. Today's material will be on the exam but we will begin tomorrow with the next assignment." By the time Slocum reached the door, the classroom was buzzing. The offending student recanted. Slocum told him the facts of the case and then grilled him for the rest of the hour. Given that story, it was little wonder that we would see a few students in the hallway with their ears pressed to the door of Slocum's class. They did not want to miss what was said but, unprepared, they were not willing to risk being called on in class.[131]*

Professor Alfred Slocum. *Courtesy of Janice Russo.*

The characters and the stories about them could go on and on. As the Francione-Thomas piece demonstrates, there's something to be said about almost everyone who has been a part of the history of Rutgers Law. And this chapter hasn't even dealt with the prodigious equal employment opportunity contributions (and elephant-like memory) of Al Blumrosen; the great legal skills and equally great raconteur's abilities of Annamay Sheppard; the remarkable private life of John Lowenthal, by day a tweedy tax professor and by night a word-class chamber musician and documentary filmmaker devoted to saving Alger Hiss's reputation; and the mind-boggling transformations of Bob Carter's body and office from overstuffed to spare and orderly and then back again.

And that's just the faculty. There's also the incredible dedication and staying power of administrators such as Linda Garbaccio and Marie Melito and the enormous contributions of newer kids on the administrative block such as Fran Bouchoux, Andy Rothman and Anita Walton. We're also all relishing the return "home" of that jack-of-all-trades (and master of all), Ron Chen, the latest in a string of Rutgers Law public advocates.

To highlight these relatively few faculty and administrators means leaving unnamed so many others who have played an important role in the first one hundred years of Rutgers Law. It is inevitable, however, when those years have to be compressed into not greatly more than a page of text per year.

The same is true, but even more so, of the generations of students. So many have gone on to enrich the legal, policy and political life of our state and nation. So many present remarkable stories of accomplishment, often in the face of great odds. One of those stories has to be told, however. If any justification is needed for selecting this one over all the other possibilities, let it be that her name is the only one that adorns the Rutgers Law building, because her classmates insisted that it happen. The story is of Ann Jennifer Smaldone, better known to everyone as A.J., class of 1977. Her courage and character still bring many of her classmates to tears. The following is excerpted from a piece written by A.J.'s classmate, Bob Goldsmith, on the occasion of the class's twenty-fifth reunion, when the law school garden was dedicated to A.J.'s memory:

> *A.J. was born after World War II and as a young child, just before the Salk vaccine, [she] contracted all three strains of polio. The chances of getting all three…were one in 10,000. The chances of surviving were one in a*

The A.J. Smaldone dedication plaque.

million. A.J. was simply one in a million. A.J. spent more than a year in an iron lung, which was a massive iron tank that would breathe for people afflicted with pulmonary polio...

A.J. was truly one of the most remarkable human beings I have ever known. To us, she never had a bad day. The polio had decimated her body, she was only 65 pounds, and she could not walk. She wrote with her right arm, but it was so weak that it stayed stationary and she moved the paper with her left hand. Throughout her life she had difficulty breathing. In fact, A.J. died in July 1980 of complications from her polio. She was deprived of the last two decades during which her classmates have achieved greatly...

A.J. was effervescent, bright, funny, warm, supportive, insightful and just simply a splendid person. At our graduation, she received an award and strode up to the podium in her electric wheelchair to a standing ovation from all of her classmates, their families and friends, as well as attending dignitaries. She touched the lives of so many. A.J. took what she had and ran with it, in a wheelchair.

On her death in 1980, we established a fund at Rutgers Law School in her honor...As the new law school building was being designed, those

The A.J. Smaldone Terrace and Garden.

close to A.J. suggested that some element be dedicated to her. At the Spring Dinner in 2000, after learning that the building had a garden, some of us immediately saw that the garden should be dedicated to A.J.'s honor. It was perfect for A.J. as long as it had daisies, her favorite flower.[132]

As Bob Goldsmith's eloquent words make clear, A.J. had a profound impact on her classmates. In her acceptance of a Distinguished Alumna Award in 2009, Ann Lesk, another classmate, acknowledged A.J.'s influence on the class of 1977. "A.J.'s determination and cheerfulness set the tone for our entire class. She made us all better lawyers."

A.J.'s influence reached far beyond her classmates and Rutgers Law, though. In the few years granted her after her graduation, A.J. became one of the country's pioneer advocates for the disabled. At the law school's graduation every year, this is recognized by the presentation of the A.J. Smaldone Award for Defending Legal Rights of the Handicapped.

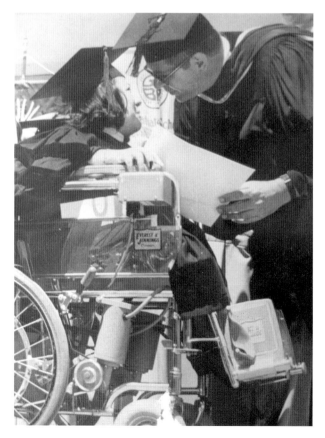

Ann Jennifer Smaldone receiving her diploma from then dean Peter Simmons.

Clearly, the story of A.J. Smaldone at Rutgers Law is a story about friendship and love as much as it is about professional accomplishment. The social and emotional dimension of Rutgers Law is especially difficult to capture. Partly that's because it's not just a story of relationships among students or among faculty. The magic of Rutgers Law has been about the crossover relationships between students and faculty. Sometimes that has been primarily professional, sometimes casually friendly and sometimes more intense. More than a few marriages have occurred between students and faculty, as is perhaps the case elsewhere.

However, it's even more than that. For substantial periods of Rutgers Law's history—and particularly from the late 1960s through the mid-1980s—there was a distinctive sense of shared purpose and commitment. There was an unusual social ease, as well. Faculty members partied with students, and they attended student dinners and other events en masse, including the decidedly ribald Libel Play, in which students parodied faculty to the delight of one and all, including the parodied faculty members. Old yearbooks have photo after photo of large numbers of faculty laughing uproariously at jokes poked at them.

One of the most memorable of the parodies was of Ruth Ginsburg as a civil procedure teacher. As a law professor, she was equally well known for both her total focus and her lack of an obvious sense of humor. The skit involved a female student, as Ruth Ginsburg, delivering a lecture on some arcane point of civil procedure as another student, from behind her, removed her clothing article by article without the pseudo Ruth noticing. The best part of the parody was the sight of Professor/Justice Ginsburg sitting in the front row roaring with laughter.

The times have changed, though. Although faculty members and students still get along well and often form lasting friendships, the dynamic is different; and it's hard to say why. Libel Plays haven't been presented for many years. Faculty members still attend some student events, most notably the MSP Banquet, the PILF Auction, Jazz for Justice and the Barristers Ball, but they don't seem to attend in anything like the same numbers. Perhaps it's because more faculty members seem to have young children at home; perhaps it's because advances in technology have made it far easier to work at home when you're not teaching; perhaps it's the broader social impact of the *Bowling Alone* phenomenon; perhaps students just aren't as interested in interacting with faculty members with the same intensity; or perhaps students are more concerned about their grades, passing the bar and getting good jobs.

Whatever the causes, it seems a real loss. Perhaps we can do something about that as we consider ways to transform Rutgers Law once again in the future. Perhaps we ought to consider resurrecting the old pub in the basement of 15 Washington Street where so many of us experienced such enjoyable interludes—or at least formally anointing McGovern's as the Rutgers Law pub. Come to think of it, maybe we've already done that on a de facto basis.

CONCLUDING WORDS

Appropriately enough, this chapter concludes with the words of students from the Rutgers Law Centennial Seminar of 2008–9, who conceived of the idea for a book and developed a first draft of it.

From the Mouths of the Students

Perhaps Rutgers Law cannot be described better than does the title to Bob Braun's recent *Star-Ledger* article, "A Century's Eccentricity at Rutgers Law School Yields Legal Greatness."[133] In part, the article describes a band of mothers who supported each other through law school's ups and downs. The school is just weird.

A crowd of students, staff and faculty at a Centennial event. *Courtesy of Shelley Kusnetz.*

Our research regularly turned up documents that required a second reading because one simply could not believe that someone had said or done what appeared on the page. Nancy Erika Smith, '80, said at the October 2008 Centennial Celebration that "Rutgers made me crazy" and that "Rutgers Law School took a chance on me and I will never ever forget it." This curious school has accomplished so much with the limited resources available to it to educate decades of graduates.

Throughout the writing of this book, it has become apparent to us that everyone seems to have a different idea of what Rutgers Law is. Many characterize the school as a progressive, public interest–oriented school that is at risk of losing its way. Others highlight current social justice and community support programs and celebrate the law school's continuing efforts in the public interest field. Still others consider it their springboard into private practice at small firms in New Jersey or at megafirms in New York City and around the country.

This book could have focused on the public interest and public service perceptions of the school—the fabled People's Electric Law School. It would

Professor Kinoy.

be understandable since graduating a successful corporate or tax lawyer just isn't as exciting as graduating a new Frank Askin to argue high-profile cases in a high court on behalf of the poor and downtrodden or a new Arthur Kinoy to be dragged out of a Congressional hearing room for standing up to runaway authority.

However, graduating an outstanding corporate, tax or bankruptcy specialist may be no less important than fighting for the rights of the underserved. Indeed, one of our graduates has demonstrated that the two are not necessarily separate paths. Elizabeth Warren, '76, was named by *Time* magazine as one of the world's one hundred most influential people. After graduating from Rutgers Law, she taught one of the school's first night classes after the program was reestablished. She went on to become a distinguished professor at Harvard Law School, vice-president of the American Law Institute and now chair of the Congressional Oversight Panel, which has responsibility for $700 billion of Troubled Asset Relief Program (TARP) funding.

Through her work in bankruptcy law, and especially her focus on middle-class financial problems, Professor Warren arguably has had far more impact on social policy than someone who specialized in a field more ostensibly public interest oriented. Could she have had such an impact on the nation and the world without the opportunities that Rutgers Law provided her? She doesn't seem to think so. In a recent statement, which provided the basis for this book's title, Elizabeth Warren expressed her great appreciation to Rutgers Law, which "took a poor kid from Oklahoma and kicked open a thousand doors for [her]."[134]

Graduates and faculty members like Elizabeth Warren sometimes tend to get lost in the history of Rutgers Law. What cannot be lost in the history of the school, however, is the notion that the school not only strives for a diverse student body but is also diverse itself. The school has educated people with many different goals, often with a budget far below its competitors. Students have perpetually walked away from graduation prepared for myriad professional opportunities.

The most remarkable thing about Rutgers Law is its capacity to change. Can you imagine any other law school literally shutting down and reevaluating its curriculum for a day because a group of students wrote a complaint? It is even harder to imagine another school drastically changing its curriculum in less than a year as a response to such a complaint. The school has started, eliminated and again opened a part-time evening program as the goals of Rutgers Law, and the political imperatives, have changed over time.

Elizabeth Warren, '76, not only one of Rutgers Law's most prominent graduates, but also one of the world's one hundred most influential people.

Originally founded on the premise that working-class people should be able to obtain a legal education, Rutgers' emphasis shifted in the mid- to late 1960s in response to racial conflicts in America. It is not clear whether either of those decisions was made to maintain a progressive social agenda. The school simply changed as society changed around it. Progressive ideas and policies are no less forward looking if they are implemented for self-preservation. Today, the racial climate in America has fortunately changed (as exemplified by the historic election of President Barack Obama), and "radical" student movements of the kind that populated the People's Electric Law School are for the most part unknown.

Currently, newly formed (and in some situations, newly accredited) law schools appear to be the loudest advocates for change in American legal education. Accordingly, such law schools have incorporated more practical than theoretical programs into their curriculum and, in some cases, have even shortened the term of study necessary to secure a law degree. Remembering that sometimes the most important change is the one not made, Rutgers Law will certainly look into these options for its own future. If history is any indication of the future, the law school will have no problem adapting to whatever society demands that it be.

It is tempting to ask if Rutgers is still the "People's Electric Law School" or if the increased financial burdens facing students have changed the very nature of the law school. In our judgment, this isn't the right question to ask. The real question should be, "Is Rutgers Law the best school that it can be for current law students and for society?"

In reality, most current applicants know little about the law school's storied past. Rather, they apply for other reasons, including relatively affordable tuition, proximity to New York City and faculty prestige. Nevertheless, carryovers from the past, when students took active roles in the surrounding community, persist.

Recently, Rutgers Law was highly ranked for public interest law. Numerous community service opportunities exist for law students, ranging from Street Law to the Domestic Violence Advocacy Project. Students who accrue at least thirty-five hours of pro bono service by participating in such activities receive a special citation on their transcripts and graduation certificates.

This, however, is not the complete picture of what the school has to offer its students. The school also has a thriving placement program for second-year summer jobs; offers many courses that are geared toward private practice, government work or individual practice; and has faculty acclaimed for work wholly unrelated to advocacy or social change. "It would be a mistake…to suggest Rutgers Law School is—or even ever was—some sort of alternative law school given over to nontraditional students. Most graduates then, and now, head for the big firms and, if possible, the big bucks—including those who might come through [the] special admissions program."[135]

New Jersey Supreme Court justice Jaynee LaVecchia, '80, perhaps described the school's pluralistic educational goals best when she said, "I knew I wanted to go to Rutgers Law School. Its reputation had preceded it. [It had a] reputation for diversity; but also a reputation for excellence."[136]

When we began to prepare our contributions for this book, some of us felt that there was a lack of information available about Rutgers Law. After completing the research, however, it appeared that there was plenty of information about the school—it was just scattered in many different places. This is to be expected from a school that has changed affiliations and grown out of its buildings as many times as Rutgers Law has. It is very likely that our research and the writing of this book have omitted parts of the school's history. That is inevitable since the law school has been so many things to so many people throughout its one-hundred-year history.

We hope, though, that we have captured enough to portray the journey that the school has made from upstart for-profit New Jersey Law School to Rutgers Law. Throughout our look at the school's past, it has become clear that Rutgers Law is not mainly about the buildings, the classes or even the affiliations. The school is really about the people who work and learn in it. We hope that the next one hundred years can be filled with as many wonderful people as the previous one hundred were.

During those one hundred years, Rutgers Law was shaped by the events that took place around it and in it. The school did not hesitate to adapt its goals, its policies and its curriculum to the times. The direction the school takes during the next one hundred years remains an exciting question. However, we believe there will continue to be some constants:

- A commitment to diversity of faculty and students and to welcoming those who might otherwise not have an opportunity to receive a high-quality legal education.
- A commitment to instilling in all its students the value of public service and of using law to improve society and the lot of those in need.
- A commitment to offering all students substantial experiential legal education opportunities.
- A commitment to a pluralistic approach to legal education and to the practice of law.
- A commitment to maintaining the highest ethical standards.

The precise way in which those commitments are assured is less important than the commitments themselves. However, we believe that Rutgers Law will continue to be a leading innovator in legal education. Throughout its history, Rutgers Law has often been a leader in the evolution of legal education. The school has struggled to accomplish many things with limited resources and throughout many periods of turmoil, with surprisingly great success. If history is an accurate predictor of the future, Rutgers Law has successful times ahead of it even if we can't predict exactly what form those successes will take. Documenting those successes will be the responsibility of future chroniclers. For now, we have done what we could.

CHAPTER 7

THE NEXT ONE HUNDRED YEARS
OF RUTGERS LAW
(2009 AND BEYOND)

Of necessity, this last chapter will predict Rutgers Law's long-term future in only the sketchiest terms. Building on the two previous chapters, which dealt with some recent challenges, this chapter will describe in some detail where Rutgers Law stands in 2009 and what the immediate future may hold.

With a prominent new dean, John Farmer,[137] who was recruited to "catapult" Rutgers Law to the top ranks of American public law schools, several major directions for the school are emerging. To a substantial degree, they are being driven by a common challenge—the inadequacy of currently available resources and the unlikelihood of the situation improving significantly if business were to continue more or less as usual.

One possible new direction involves a fundamental restructuring of the relationship between the law school and university. A number of public law schools, confronted with similar, if less dramatic, problems, have moved toward a form of privatization. The furthest-reaching example is the University of Virginia's Financial Self-Sufficiency Plan, under which the law school gets relatively broad discretion over its tuition rates and other budgetary elements and gets to keep the great bulk of revenue it generates through tuition and otherwise. In exchange, it pays the university a "tax" for continued use of the University of Virginia name.[138]

Other public law schools have negotiated different deals with their universities, but the common element is an ability to retain a greater portion of law school–generated revenue. Negotiating such a deal is not easy, however, since over the years many law schools, private as well as public, have been "cash cows" for their universities, with law school–generated revenues helping to support other less lucrative units.

In these difficult economic times, with many public universities becoming desperately short of funding, negotiating a favorable deal for the law school is especially challenging. At least at Rutgers Law, though, there seems no alternative—certainly not if the law school is going to be catapulted upward.

Without going into great detail, a few statistics drawn from the most recent ABA compilation of annual questionnaire data submitted by all law schools should suffice to dramatize the situation:

- Rutgers Law's expenditure per Full Time Equivalent (FTE) student is $30,980, as compared to an average of $48,782 for four "peer" public law schools in the same general geographic area (Connecticut, Penn State [Dickinson], Maryland and Temple).
- That translates into a substantially smaller faculty; a substantially higher faculty teaching load; and a higher student-faculty ratio as compared to the peer schools.
- Not surprisingly, given those numbers, Rutgers Law's USNWR ranking is 87, as compared to an average of 56 for the peer schools.

Surprisingly, the explanation is not that we charge significantly less tuition and, therefore, generate significantly less revenue. Our in-state tuition actually is slightly higher than the average of our four peer public law schools ($23,007 as compared to $22,306), and our out-of-state tuition is only slightly lower than the peer group average ($32,777 as compared to $33,236). Therefore, the explanation must be that the peer public law schools get to keep a significantly larger share of their tuition revenue, they receive significantly larger amounts of state and university support, they raise and get to keep significantly larger amounts of entrepreneurial and fundraising revenue or some combination of those elements.

These resource disparities also affect our library. In 1985, we were spending significantly more than a somewhat different peer group (Connecticut, Maryland, Florida, Indiana–Bloomington, Cardozo, Pittsburgh and Rutgers–Camden). By 2007, we were spending barely half as much as they were. Yet, as a current example of how Rutgers Law has continued to do more with less, in its March 2010 issue the *National Jurist* ranked the library forty-seven in its list of the fifty best law libraries out of 198 surveyed.

If one looks further afield at other public law schools, one finds that, although a number are significantly smaller than Rutgers by student enrollment, their staffing is far richer. For example, the University of Washington Law School has an enrollment of 534 FTE as compared to 736 at Rutgers Law, yet it has a far larger tenured and tenure-track faculty (54 as compared to 35), slightly larger clinical faculty (11 as compared to 10), far larger library faculty and staff (26 as compared to 12) and vastly larger administration (64 as compared to 14).

Until detailed comparisons of these sorts were made during the fall of 2009, the Rutgers Law community was unaware of the full extent to which it was under-resourced. It led to a renewed sense of pride at how much we have been able to do with so relatively little but also to a strong commitment to address the problem.

Given the severe economic plight confronting both the nation and the state of New Jersey, Rutgers Law will have to find some out-of-the-box solutions to its resource dilemma, as it has found ingenious solutions to other, past challenges.

In addition to restructuring the relationship between the law school and the university, a process just initiated in the winter of 2009, Rutgers Law will have to develop major new sources of funding. One is the time-honored approach of increased alumni and other philanthropic support. Another newer approach for law schools is to become more entrepreneurial. One especially promising entrepreneurial possibility grows out of New Jersey's new mandatory continuing legal education requirement. Under the court rule, Rutgers Law and the other two New Jersey law schools are "approved providers." Dean Farmer has hired an experienced hand at continuing legal education to head up Rutgers Law's effort.

It is tempting to consider increasing tuition and fees as another means of augmenting Rutgers Law's revenue and resources, but that approach may prove complicated, controversial or even counterproductive. There are both moral and pragmatic concerns. Putting an even greater burden on students will tend to advantage those with easy access to funding and disadvantage those of modest means. Historically, the latter group has been Rutgers Law's backbone.

Moreover, as a pragmatic matter, it is unclear whether this approach will work. As the legal job market has begun to contract, law students and applicants alike have begun to reconsider the wisdom of choosing a legal education, especially one for which they have to go deeply in debt. Increasing tuition and fees will only heighten their concerns.

Over its first one hundred years, Rutgers Law has periodically experienced such ebb and flow based on recessions, world wars and other crises. It has always survived and bounced back, often reinventing itself in the process. In the longer term, that is likely to happen again, but in the shorter term, there may well be some serious stresses.

One curiosity about public legal education in New Jersey is that, unlike most state law schools across the country, there are two Rutgers law schools and neither is located on the university's main campus in New Brunswick. As the earlier chapters describe, there are old historical explanations and continuing political reasons for that unusual configuration. Prior efforts to combine the two law schools never got far. But that was then; now and in the future, a different dynamic may emerge.

Another less dramatic reconfiguration may involve the part-time evening program. Clearly, it is an added drain on limited resources, and at least in the short term, there may not be as much demand or justification for it. Moreover, the legislative mandate that reestablished it in 1975, over substantial faculty opposition, probably no longer has legal force, since it was accomplished by several consecutive annual appropriations acts but not by permanent legislation. There are other transformative possibilities suggested by the previous chapter. One has to do with an increased linkage between legal education and the legal profession. Over the years, that has led to sometimes serious discussion about reducing formal law school education to two years and restructuring the third year as a bridge to practice. Related to that are yearlong externship programs, such as Northeastern's, in which law students are in residence only for two years.

Still another transformative possibility, frightening to some, is the advance of technology and its implications for legal education. In Rutgers Law's relatively new building, there is a classroom for "distance learning." It has been used only occasionally. The CALI program (Computer Assisted Legal Instruction) has been around for decades, but it also has been little used at Rutgers Law. At the outer edge of technology and legal education is the recent establishment of several unaccredited virtual law schools, inspired by the University of Phoenix's success (at least financially). Still other ideas surface regularly about finding an educationally effective and cost-efficient way to combine live and electronic instruction. After all, if the physical barriers to instruction can be broken through, at least in part, and the costs reduced, the pool of students can be increased dramatically.

All of these possibilities, and many others not yet on the radar screen, await Rutgers Law during its next one hundred years. Although the form of legal education in the future may defy our current view (or wind up looking much like today's version), many of the same challenges that have confronted Rutgers Law during its first one hundred years are likely to persist.

Can Rutgers Law continue to serve students who are not—by birth, upbringing or socioeconomic status—programmed to become lawyers? Can Rutgers Law continue to engage in the difficult balancing act, with never quite enough resources, of playing a leading role in promoting diversity, instilling in students public interest and public service values and providing experiential learning opportunities through legal clinics while at the same time seeking to prepare most of its graduates for the private practice of law, often in small firms, and to open their minds to legal theory and jurisprudence?

Just framing these questions makes it obvious how difficult it has been for much of the past one hundred years, and how difficult it will be for much of the next one hundred years, for Rutgers Law to keep all of these balls in the air. Yet, miraculously, in taking stock after the first one hundred years, it does appear that, despite periodic bobbles and imperfections, the task has been accomplished. Rutgers Law has managed to "open a thousand doors" for many thousands of graduates, a good number of whom would never have gotten the opportunity without this imperfect but quite wonderful place.

RUTGERS LAW'S CENTENNIAL TIMELINE

1908

The New Jersey Law School (NJLS) opens as a for-profit law school in the Prudential Insurance Building on October 5. Founders include President Richard D. Currier (the first president), Dean Percival Barnard and Charles M. Mason, as a member of the faculty.

The school moves to its own building at 33 East Park Street in December of its first year of existence.

1909

The New Jersey Board of Bar Examiners recognizes NJLS as school of "established reputation." As a consequence, completion of an eighteen-month course of study at NJLS would satisfy half of the three-year clerkship requirement for admission to the New Jersey Bar.

1910

Laura Mayo Wilson is the first woman to graduate.

1913

The New Jersey Board of Education approves NJLS to grant degrees.

NJLS's curriculum is extended from two to three years.

1914
NJLS Press publishes its first casebook, *Cases on Torts*, by Currier and Bates. High school graduation becomes a requirement for admission.

1915
Calvin McClelland becomes the first blind professor.

1918
Elizabeth Blume (class of 1911) becomes the first woman to defend a client for murder.

1925
Two years of college work is phased in as a requirement for law school admission.

1926
Mercer Beasley School of Law is founded—located first at 60 Park Place and then on the sixth floor of an industrial office building at 1060 Broad Street.

1927
The pre-legal department of NJLS is established.

1929
The Seth Boyden School of Business is founded by NJLS.

1930
NJLS sells its building at 33 East Park Street and relocates to 40 Rector Street.

NJLS acquires nonprofit status.

Dana College is founded and absorbs the pre-legal department of NJLS.

1934
The Mercer Beasley School of Law and the Newark Institute of Arts & Sciences merge into the University of Newark, located at 17–25 Academy Street.

1936
NJLS and the Seth Boyden School of Business merge into Dana College.

1939

A four-year, part-time program is initiated.

1941

The University of Newark School of Law gains American Bar Association (ABA) accreditation.

1946

The University of Newark becomes part of Rutgers University.

The law school moves to 37 Washington Street.

Legal clinic practice by students in criminal courts begins.

1950

William B. Widnall (class of 1931) elected to the U.S. Congress, where he served for twenty-four years.

Appellate Moot Court Program is initiated.

1955

Clarence Clyde Ferguson Jr. becomes the first African American professor.

The evening program is discontinued.

1956

The law school moves to 53 Washington Street.

1961

Richard J. Hughes (class of 1931) is elected governor of New Jersey.

1962

Eva Hanna Morreale (Hanks) becomes first female professor.

Edward J. Patten (class of 1926) becomes a member of Congress and serves until 1980.

1963

Ruth Bader Ginsburg joins the faculty, teaching at the law school until 1972.

1964

Arthur Kinoy joins the faculty.

1965

The law school moves to the newly constructed Ackerson Hall at 180 University Avenue.

1968

The Minority Student Program is established.

1969

The Rutgers–Newark Black Organization of Students takes over Conklin Hall for seventy-two hours to protest the lack of diversity at the University.

The Association of Black Law Students publishes "Indictment of the Rutgers Law School Community," calling for an overhaul of the law school curriculum. This led to the establishment of the Tripartite Commission, which proposed a radical curricular overhaul.

The Administrative Process Project becomes the first curricular clinical program.

1970

The Constitutional Litigation Clinic is established by Professor Frank Askin (class of 1966).

The Urban Legal Clinic is established.

1971

José Cabranes becomes the first Latino professor.

1975

The evening program is reestablished.

1977

Peggy Cooper Davis becomes the first female African American professor.

The Women's Rights Litigation Clinic is successful in *Tomkins v. PSE&G*, 568 F.2d 1044, the first Third Circuit decision to recognize sexual harassment as gender discrimination.

1979

The law school moves to 15 Washington Street.

The Constitutional Litigation Clinic wins its case involving the FBI investigation of a high school student, *Paton v. LaPrade*, 471 F. Supp. 166 (DNJ).

1982

Alan Karcher (class of 1967) becomes speaker of the New Jersey Assembly.

1983

Right to Choose v. Byrne, 91 N.J. 287, with Professors Nadine Taub and Louis Raveson for the plaintiffs-respondents, establishes that the State of New Jersey must pay for Medicaid abortions for indigent women.

1987

Ronald Chen becomes the first Asian-American professor.

1988

Initial substantive decision is issued in *Abbott v. Burke*. The case was brought by Marilyn Morheuser (class of 1973) as director of the Education Law Center, a public interest law project founded in 1973 by Professor Paul Tractenberg; opinion was written by Steven LeFelt, ALJ (class of 1965).

1993

Robert Menendez (class of 1979) is elected to the U.S. House of Representatives from New Jersey. He is elected to the U.S. Senate in 2006.

Hazel O'Leary (class of 1966) is appointed U.S. secretary of energy.

1994

The mall leafleting case *New Jersey Coalition Against War in the Middle East v. J.M.B. Realty Corp.*, 138 N.J. 326, with Professor Frank Askin representing the ACLU, establishes that the free speech provisions of the state constitution exceed those of the First Amendment.

1998

Constitutional Litigation Clinic victory establishing customary international law as basis for suit in *Jama v. U.S. Immigration & Naturalization Service*, 22 F.Supp.2d 353 (DNJ). See also 343 F.Supp.2d 338 (DNJ 2004).

1999

The Loan Repayment Assistance Program is created.

Appellate Division presiding judge Virginia Long (class of 1966) becomes an associate justice of the New Jersey Supreme Court.

2000

The law school moves to the new Center for Law and Justice at 123 Washington Street.

Jaynee LaVecchia (class of 1979) becomes an associate justice of the New Jersey Supreme Court. She had been New Jersey Commissioner of Banking and Insurance.

Professor Jon Dubin is co-counsel in the successful appeal of *Sims v. Apfel*, 530 U.S. 103, a Social Security disability case, and the U.S. Supreme Court cites Dubin's article in its opinion.

2006

Ronald Chen (class of 1983) becomes a New Jersey public advocate.

2007

Students organize the school's first annual "Pro Bono Day," on which law students coordinate and participate in daylong volunteer projects in the local community.

SAMPLING OF RUTGERS LAW SCHOOL CENTENNIAL YEAR EVENTS

September 9, 2008: School-wide Centennial celebration sponsored by Rutgers–Newark School of Law.

October 16, 2008: "Perspectives on Obama, Race and the Law," symposium sponsored by *Rutgers Race and the Law Review.*

October 20, 2008: "Celebrating a 100-Year Tradition of Diversity: Reflections on Its Success," hosted by the Centennial Seminar.

October 24, 2008: "Iraq at the Crossroads: Protecting Refugees, Rescuing Our Allies, and Empowering Iraqi Law," symposium hosted by the *Rutgers Law Record.*

November 5, 2008: "'The Morning After': Issues Facing the Post-Election Nation," and presentation of the Eric R. Neisser Public Interest Award sponsored by the Eric R. Neisser Public Interest Program.

February 13, 2009: "Role of Women and the Law School in Reshaping American Law."

February 25, 2009: "The Repatriation of African Art: Art Scholars and Art Lawyers Discuss African Nations' Fight to Retrieve Their Art Treasures," sponsored by the Art Law Society, Office of Career Services, Association of Black Law Students, Asian Pacific-American Law Students Association and International Law Society at Rutgers School of Law–Newark, as well as by New Jersey Volunteer Lawyers for the Arts.

March 6, 2009: "The Gender Dimensions of Terrorism: How Terrorism Impacts the Lives of Women," annual symposium, sponsored by the *Women's Rights Law Reporter.*

March 26, 2009: "Changing Times, Changing Minds," sponsored by the New Jersey Supreme Court Committee on Women in the Courts.

April 1, 2009: "Live from Death Row," presented by the Human Rights Forum.

April 2, 2009: "A Symposium on E-Discovery and Its Impact on Corporate Governance and Litigation" sponsored by the *Rutgers Business Law Journal.*

April 3, 2009: "The Legacy of Arthur Kinoy and the Inspirational and Collaborative Dimensions of Clinical Legal Education: Celebrating 40 Years of Clinical Legal Education at Rutgers–Newark" sponsored by the Rutgers–Newark School of Law legal clinics.

April 17, 2009: "A Legal Education Prospectus: Law Schools & Emerging Frontiers in Curriculum, Lawyering, and Social Justice" sponsored by the *Rutgers Law Review* and featuring an afternoon session on instilling in students public interest values conducted by the Centennial Seminar.

RUTGERS LAW'S "FIRSTS"

First law school in the state, New Jersey Law School, opens (1908).

First female graduate: Laura Mayo Wilson (1910).

First issue of *New Jersey Law Review* is published (1915).

First blind professor joins faculty: Calvin McClelland (1915).

First female attorney in New Jersey to defend a client for murder: Elizabeth Blume Silverstein, class of 1911 (1918).

First issue of New Jersey Law yearbook, *Legacy*, and student newspaper, *Barrister*, published (1927).

First graduate to become dean: George S. Harris, class of 1922 (1928).

First issue of Mercer Beasley yearbook, *Pandects*, is published (1929).

First issue of *Mercer Beasley Law Review* is published (1932).

First issue of *University of Newark Law Review* is published (1936).

First law students permitted to engage in legal clinic practice in criminal courts (1946).

First issue of *Rutgers Law Review* is published (1947).

First Appellate Moot Court Program is established (1950).

First African American professor joins faculty: Clarence Clyde Ferguson (1955).

First female professor joins faculty: Eva Hanna Hanks (née Morreale) (1962).

First Minority Student Program is established (1968).

First law review in the United States focusing on society's interaction with computers and emerging technologies, the *Rutgers Computer and Technology Law Journal*, is established (1969).

First law reform clinic in a U.S. law school, the Constitutional Litigation Clinic, is established (1970).

First Latino professor joins faculty: José Cabranes (1971).

First law journal in the United States to focus exclusively on women's rights, the *Women's Rights Law Reporter*, is established with then professor Ruth Bader Ginsburg as co-founder (1971).

First public interest law center exclusively devoted to representing parents and students, the Education Law Center, is established (1973).

First U.S. law school to enroll more than 50 percent women (1977).

First African American female professor joins faculty: Peggy Cooper Davis (1977).

First Asian-American professor joins faculty: Ronald Chen, class of 1983 (1987).

First Animal Rights Law Clinic is founded (1990).

First former faculty member is appointed to the U.S. Supreme Court: Ruth Bader Ginsburg (1993).

First general online law review, *Rutgers Law Record*, is published (1996).

First issue of *Rutgers Race & The Law Review* is published (1998).

First issue of *Rutgers Bankruptcy Law Review* is published (name later changed to *Rutgers Business Law Review*) (1998).

First lieutenant governor of New Jersey elected: Kim Guadagno, a legal research and writing instructor at Rutgers Law (2009).

RUTGERS LAW'S DEANS

Percival Bernard	1908–1909
Charles Meeks Mason	1909–1928
George Stiles Harris	1928–1936
Spaulding Frazier	1936–1940
George Stiles Harris	1940–1951
Alfred Comstock Clapp	1951–1953
Lehan Kent Tunks	1953–1962
C. Willard Heckel	1963–1970
James C.N. Paul	1970–1973
C. Willard Heckel (acting)	1973–1974
Alfred Blumrosen (acting)	1974–1975
Peter Simmons	1975–1993
Roger I. Abrams	1993–1998
Eric R. Neisser (acting)	1998–1999
Stuart L. Deutsch	1999–2009
John J. Farmer Jr.	2009–

RUTGERS LAW'S HOMES

Prudential Insurance Building, fourth floor	1908 (October–December)
33 East Park Street, Victorian town house (renovated)	1908–1921
33 East Park Street, Gothic building (newly built)	1921–1931
40 Rector Street, Ballantine Brewery factory (renovated)	1930–1947
37 Washington Street, Ballantine mansion (renovated)	1947–1956
53 Washington Street, YWCA (renovated)	1956–1965
180 University Avenue, Ackerson Hall (newly built)	1965–1979
15 Washington Street, S.I. Newhouse Center for Law and Justice (renovated)	1979–1999
123 Washington Street, Center for Law and Justice (newly built)	2000–

APPENDIX V

RUTGERS LAW'S PROMINENT FORMER FACULTY—A SELECTION

Allan Axelrod
Vicki Been
Alfred Blumrosen
William Bratton
Alexander Brooks
Victor Brudney
José Cabranes
Norman Cantor
Robert Carter
Marvin Chirelstein
Richard Chused
Alfred Clapp
Felix Cohen
Julius Cohen
Sherry Colb
Drucilla Cornell
Thomas Cowan
Jerome Culp
Charles Davenport
Peggy Cooper Davis
C. Clyde Ferguson Jr.
Vincent Fiordalisi
Carl Fulda
Ruth Bader Ginsburg

Suzanne Goldberg
Wendy Gordon
John Graham
David Haber
Willard Heckel
Eli Jarmel
Nicholas Katzenbach
Arthur Kinoy
Robert Knowlton
Arthur Lewis
John Lowenthal
Saul Mendlovitz
Gerry Moran
Eva Morreale Hanks
Eric Neisser
John Payne
Sidney Posel
David Rice
Dorothy Roberts
Mark Roe
Morris Schnitzer
Alan Schwarz
Annamay Sheppard
Richard Singer

Alfred Slocum
J. Allen Smith
David Stoffer
Malcolm Talbott
Nadine Taub
Jane Zuckerman

APPENDIX VI

RUTGERS LAW'S PROMINENT ALUMNI—A SELECTION

Name	Best Known As	Graduated
Harold A. Ackerman	U.S. District Court Judge	1951
Frank Askin	Professor, Rutgers Law–Newark	1966
Marilyn Askin	Prominent Elder Law Lawyer	1970
Cynthia Augustine	Senior Vice-President, Time Warner	1982
Richard H. Bagger	Served in both houses of New Jersey legislature	1986
George H. Barlow	U.S. District Court Judge	1948
Lawrence E. Bathgate II	Managing Partner, Bathgate, Wegener & Wolf	1964
Ed Baumer	Chair, World Wide Super Senior Sports	1937
Dorothea Beane	Professor, Stetson University College of Law	1977
Candice Beinecke	Chair, Hughes, Hubbard & Reed, LLP	1970
Melvyn H. Bergstein	Partner, Walter, Hayden & Brogan, P.A.	1963
Marc E. Berson	Chair, Fidelco Group & Newark Bears	1968

Name	Best Known As	Graduated
Fannie B. Besser	Poverty Law Specialist	1920
Nancy Biberman	Founder, Women's Housing and Economic Development Corporation	1973
Maureen S. Binetti	Partner, Wilentz, Goldman & Spitzer	1982
Vincent P. Biunno	U.S. District Court Judge	1937
Elizabeth Blume Silverstein	First woman in New Jersey to handle defense in a murder trial	1911
Gordon Canfield	U.S. House of Representatives	1924
Michael P. Carroll	New Jersey Assemblyman	1983
Ida Castro	U.S. Equal Employment Opportunity Commission Chair	1982
James Ciancia	New Jersey Appellate Division Judge	1969
Joseph Charles Jr.	New Jersey Assemblyman, State Senator	1969
Ronald Chen	New Jersey Public Advocate	1983
R. Benjamin Cohen	New Jersey Superior Court Judge	1969
Michael R. Cole	Prominent Litigator	1970
Claude M. Coleman	New Jersey Superior Court Judge	1977
Rudy B. Coleman	New Jersey Appellate Division Judge	1974
Frederick Colie	New Jersey Supreme Court Justice	1921
Kevin J. Collins	Investment Banking Authority	1964
Ermine I. Conley	New Jersey Appellate Division Judge	1971
Anthony R. Coscia	Chair, Port Authority of New York–New Jersey	1984
Mary C. Cuff	New Jersey Appellate Division Judge	1973

Rutgers Law's Prominent Alumni—A Selection

Name	Best Known As	Graduated
Robert E. Cowen	U.S. Appellate Court Third Circuit	1958
Okianer Christian Dark	Professor and Associate Dean, Howard University Law School	1979
Susan Davis	International Brotherhood of Teamsters	1981
Peter Doyne	New Jersey Superior Court Judge	1976
Naomi G. Eichen	New Jersey Appellate Division Judge	1974
Marianne Espinosa	New Jersey Superior Court Judge	1974
Zulima V. Farber	New Jersey Attorney General, New Jersey Public Advocate	1974
Mahlon L. Fast	New Jersey Superior Court Judge	1958
Andrew T. Fede	Author, Litigator	1982
Julius A. Feinberg	New Jersey Superior Court Judge	1937
W. Raymond Felton	Author, Litigator	1981
Jeffrey Fogel	Director, Center for Constitutional Rights	1969
Samuel J. Foosaner	Prominent Tax Attorney	1934
John J. Francis	New Jersey Supreme Court Justice	1925
Louis J. Freeh	U.S. FBI Director	1974
Walter J. Freund	New Jersey Appellate Division Judge	1921
Bernard Freamon	Professor, Seton Hall Law School	1974
Angelo J. Genova	Prominent Labor and Employment Lawyer	1978
Nia H. Gill	New Jersey State Senator	1975
Meryl A.G. Gonchar	Prominent Land Use Lawyer	1981
Barry S. Goodman	Prominent Public Interest Lawyer	1977
Arthur M. Greenbaum	Prominent Real Estate Lawyer	1950

Name	Best Known As	Graduated
Roxanne J. Gregory	General Counsel, Southern Christian Leadership	1979
Edward Gross	Executive Director, New Jersey Turnpike Authority	1963
David L. Harris	Prominent Litigator	1979
George S. Harris	Professor and Dean, New Jersey Law School	1922
James M. Harvey	New Jersey Appellate Division Judge	1964
C. Willard Heckel	Dean, Rutgers Law–Newark	1940
Wade Henderson	CEO, Leadership Conference on Civil Rights	1973
Lennox Hinds	Professor, Rutgers University	1972
William Hodes	Professor, Indiana University School of Law	1969
Mary Beth Hogan	Partner, Debevoise & Plimpton, LLP	1990
Jeffery D. Hsi	Partner, Edwards, Angell, Palmer & Dodge, LLP	1997
Richard J. Hughes	New Jersey Governor, New Jersey Supreme Court Chief Justice	1931
Burton J. Ironson	New Jersey Superior Court Judge	1953
Irene James	Prominent Litigator	1984
Barry Kamins	President, Association of Bar of City of New York	1968
Alan Karcher	New Jersey Assembly Speaker, Author	1967
Howard H. Kestin	New Jersey Appellate Division Judge	1962
Kevin Kiernan	Prominent Employment Lawyer	1973
Harriet F. Klein	New Jersey Superior Court Judge	1973

Name	Best Known As	Graduated
Gerald Krovatin	Prominent Criminal Defense Lawyer	1977
George H. Kugler	New Jersey Attorney General	1953
Ellen B. Kulka	General Counsel, U.S. Resolution Trust Corporation	1970
Aaron Lasser	Vice-Dean, Mercer Beasley School of Law	1919
Jaynee LaVecchia	New Jersey Supreme Court Justice	1979
Steven L. Lefelt	New Jersey Appellate Division Judge	1965
Ann B. Lesk	President, New York County Lawyers Association	1977
Betty Lester	New Jersey Superior Court Judge	1971
Donna E. Lieberman	Executive Director, New York Civil Liberties Union	1973
Martin J. Loftus	Prominent Labor Lawyer	1933
Marilyn Loftus	New Jersey Appellate Division Judge	1961
Virginia M. Long	New Jersey Supreme Court Justice	1966
Mark Lopez	Senior Staff, ACLU National Prison Project	1985
Clinton Lyons	President and CEO, National Legal Aid & Defender Association	1971
John R. MacKay	Author, Prominent Business Lawyer	1965
Harry A. Margolis	New Jersey Superior Court Judge	1953
William J. Martini	U.S. Congressman	1972
Jeff S. Masin	Deputy Director, New Jersey Office of Administrative Law	1971

Name	Best Known As	Graduated
Cynthia A. Matheke	Prominent Medical Malpractice Lawyer	1973
John A. Matthews	New Jersey Assembly, U.S. Commissioner	1910
Robert A. Matthews	New Jersey Superior Court Judge	1953
Cathe D. McAuliffe	Prominent Elder Law Lawyer	1979
Cornelius A. McGlennon	U.S. Congressman	1915
H. Curtis Meanor	U.S. District Court Judge	1955
Joseph Melillo	Newark Councilman	1941
Robert Menendez	U.S. Congressman, Senator	1979
Herman D. Michels	New Jersey Appellate Division Judge	1953
Paul S. Miller	General Counsel, Pfizer	1962
A. Harry Moore	New Jersey Governor, U.S. Senator	1922
Marilyn J. Morheuser	Executive Director, Education Law Center	1973
Frederick Morton Jr.	Senior Vice-President, MTV Networks	1993
Sybil R. Moses	First Female Assignment Judge in New Jersey	1974
Neil M. Mullin	Prominent Employment Lawyer	1979
Patricia Nachtigal	Managing Attorney, Ingersoll-Rand	1976
Oswald G. Nelson	Star of *The Adventures of Ozzie and Harriet*	1930
Edward Nusbaum	Prominent Family Lawyer	1973
Hazel O'Leary	U.S. Secretary of Energy	1966
Dean J. Paranicas	Vice-President, Becton Dickinson & Company	1976

Rutgers Law's Prominent Alumni—A Selection

Name	Best Known As	Graduated
Lorraine Parker	New Jersey Appellate Division Judge	1980
Morris Pashman	New Jersey Supreme Court Justice	1935
Florence R. Peskoe	First Female Clerk, New Jersey Supreme Court	1968
S. Joseph Picillo	Executive Director, New Jersey Institute for Continuing Legal Education	1971
Nicholas Politan	U.S. District Court Judge	1960
Cathy J. Pollak-Rosner	Prominent Family Lawyer	1976
Annette M. Quijano	New Jersey State Assemblywoman	1991
Lyle Preslar	Musician	2007
Sylvia Pressler	New Jersey Appellate Division Judge, Author	1959
Joseph Quinn	Colorado Supreme Court Justice	1961
Oliver Quinn	Vice-President, Prudential	1975
Louis Raveson	Professor, Rutgers Law–Newark	1976
Richard J. Rawson	General Counsel, Lucent Technologies	1977
Alberto Rivas	Partner, Lite, DePalma, Greenberg & Rivas	1985
Lewis J. Robinson Jr.	General Counsel, Travelers Property Casualty	1973
Peter W. Rodino Jr.	U.S. Congressman	1937
Samuel Saiber	Prominent Trusts, Estates, Taxation Lawyer	1928
Esther Salas	U.S. Magistrate Judge	1994
Susan Scarola	Groundbreaking Female Attorney	1976
Robert C. Schachter	Prominent Real Estate Lawyer	1972

Name	Best Known As	Graduated
Everett M. Scherer	Partner, Riker Danzig, Scherer	1926
Michael Sherman	Prominent Business Lawyer	1977
Annamay T. Sheppard	Professor, Rutgers Law–Newark	1958
Murray G. Simon	New Jersey Superior Court Judge	1948
Gary N. Skoloff	Prominent Family Lawyer	1958
Alfred A. Slocum	Professor, Rutgers Law, New Jersey Public Advocate	1970
Nancy E. Smith	Prominent Employment Lawyer	1980
William F. Smith	U.S. Appellate Court Third Circuit Judge	1929
Yvonne Smith-Segars	New Jersey Public Defender	1984
Kathleen A. Soled	Vice-President and General Counsel, American Eagle Air	1987
H. Theodore Sorg	Professor, New Jersey Law School	1912
L. Grace Spencer	New Jersey State Assemblywoman	1996
Arnold M. Stein	New Jersey Superior Court Judge	1957
C. Gregory Stewart	General Counsel, U.S. Equal Employment Opportunity Commission	1981
Randolph M. Subryan	New Jersey Superior Court Judge	1980
Herbert H. Tate Sr.	Cultural Attaché to Korea	1935
Herbert H. Tate Jr.	President, New Jersey Board of Public Utilities	1978
John P. Thurber	Founder, Trenton Office of Policy Studies	1982
Ivelisse Torres	New Jersey Public Defender	1977
Robert G. Torricelli	U.S. Senator	1977
Harry Towe	U.S. Congressman	1925
Luis Valentin	New Jersey's First Hispanic Prosecutor	1989

Rutgers Law's Prominent Alumni—A Selection

Name	Best Known As	Graduated
Lois Van Deusen	Managing Partner, McCarter & English, LLP	1977
Stanley C. Van Ness	New Jersey Public Advocate	1963
Walter Van Riper	Attorney General of New Jersey	1915
Jennifer Velez	Commissioner, New Jersey Deptartment Human Services	1996
Harry J. Volk	Chair, Union Bank of California	1930
Albert Lincoln Vreeland	U.S. Congressman	1925
Elizabeth Warren	Professor, Harvard Law School, Chair, COP	1976
Vincent Warren	Executive Director, Center for Constitutional Rights	1993
Barbara B. Wecker	New Jersey Appellate Division Judge	1974
Alvin Weiss	New Jersey Superior Court Judge	1953
Lawrence Weiss	New Jersey Superior Court Judge	1960
Marsha Wenk	Legal Director, ACLU New Jersey	1987
William B. Widnall	U.S. Congressman	1931
Hubert Williams	President, Police Foundation	1974
Freda L. Wolfson	U.S. District Court Judge	1979
Alfred Wolin	U.S. District Court Judge	1959
Alan L. Zegas	Prominent Criminal Defense Lawyer	1981
Homer Zink	New Jersey Assembly, New Jersey Senate	1910

Notes

Acknowledgements

1. Braun, "Success and Influence," *Star-Ledger*, June 22, 2009.

Chapter 1

2. Askin, *Defending Rights*; Kinoy, *Rights on Trial*.
3. *Rutgers Law Review* 51, Rutgers School of Thought, Symposium 1999 (1999): 777 *et seq.*
4. Francione and Thomas, "The Wind Was at Our Backs," 471.
5. Rutgers–Newark, "100 Years, 100 Milestones."

Chapter 2

6. Much of this chapter is drawn from Harold S. Wechsler's excellent paper "Brewing Bachelors: The History of the University of Newark," which was commissioned by Rutgers–Newark chancellor Steven Diner. See also Consalus, "History of Legal Education."
7. Calman, *Upsala College*, 52, 53. In 1924, Upsala moved from Kenilworth to East Orange, where it remained until it became defunct in 1995.
8. Ibid., 52.
9. Ibid., 53.
10. Rutgers–Newark, Records of the New Jersey Law School.

11. Currier, Letter to the Editor.
12. Rutgers–Newark, Records of the New Jersey Law School.
13. Currier, Letter to the Editor.
14. Wechsler, "Brewing Bachelors," 7.
15. See Denning, *Cultural Front*.
16. Rutgers–Newark, Records of the New Jersey Law School.
17. Ibid.
18. Ibid.
19. Ibid.
20. Ibid.
21. Ibid.
22. Wechsler, "Brewing Bachelors," 5.
23. Rutgers–Newark, Records of the New Jersey Law School. Tuition revenue for September 1934 was reported as $841.
24. Wechsler, "Brewing Bachelors," 12.
25. Ibid., 16.
26. Rutgers–Newark, Mercer Beasley.
27. Siracusa, "Rutgers University School of Law," dedication, 32.
28. Rutgers–Newark, Graduation Statistics, 1909–1950.
29. Rutgers–Newark, Analysis of Law School Enrollment, 1946.

Chapter 3

30. Rutgers–Newark, Records of the New Jersey Law School.
31. Rutgers–Newark, "An Account of the Situation."
32. Ibid.
33. *Newark Evening News*, March 21, 1959.
34. Tunks, Letter, 1955.
35. Rutgers–Newark, Memo on Night Law School, 1955.
36. Ibid.
37. Rutgers–Newark, Committee on Planning and Development, 1958.
38. Lloyd, "Arthur Kinoy."
39. Lewis, "Address to the Faculty."
40. Rutgers–Newark, Newark Legal Services Project.
41. Ibid.
42. Rutgers–Newark, Records of the New Jersey Law School.
43. Rutgers–Newark, Faculty Update.
44. U.S. Census Bureau, "Newark City, New Jersey."
45. Gitlin, *Sixties*, 246.

46. Rutgers–Newark, "Newark Riots, 1967."

47. Askin, "In 1967, Echoes of Newark in Plainfield."

48. Reeves, "Hatred and Pity Mix."

49. Herman, ed., *Detroit and Newark Riots.*

50. *New York Times*, "C. Willard Heckel."

51. Waggoner, "Malcolm Talbott."

CHAPTER 4

52. McCormick, *Black Student Protest Movement.*

53. Talbott, Press Release. Many BOS demands were responded to by highlighting programs or situations that were already in place or due to start. The school capitulated to all of the other demands, except those that took control of academic standards away from the faculty.

54. Rutgers–Newark, World Order Models Project.

55. Perez, "Doing Battle With Bakke," 1.

56. Heckel, Letter to Dean Russell Fairbanks.

57. Rutgers–Newark, September 1968 Plan.

58. Lefcourt, ed., *Law Against the People*, 236–38.

59. Ibid.

60. Ibid., 240.

61. Ibid., 237.

62. Ibid., 241.

63. Ibid., 243.

64. Ibid., 233–34.

65. Ibid., 244.

66. Ibid., 249–50.

67. Timoney, "Rutgers School of Law–Newark," 635, 642. See also Nixon, "Reflections on a Century-Long Tradition," 2.

68. For information about the "pre-clinical programs at Rutgers Law," see *Rutgers Law Bulletin*, School of Law, 1947–1948 through 1971–1972.

69. Administrative Process Project of Rutgers Law School, Enforcing Fair Housing Laws: Apartments in White Suburbia (July 1970); Administrative Process Project of Rutgers Law School & N.J. Div. on Civil Rights, Enforcing Equality in Housing and Employment through State Civil Rights Laws 1969–1972 (July 1972).

70. *Bronze Shields, Inc. v. New Jersey Department of Civil Service*, 488 F.Supp. 723 (DNJ 1980), *aff'd in part, rev'd in part & remanded*, 667 F.2d 1074 (Third Circuit 1981), *certiorari denied*, 458 U.S. 1122 (1982).

71. At the October 20, 2008 Centennial program on diversity, a number of speakers who wound up in prestigious mainstream legal positions underscored that point, none more powerfully than Ann Lesk, '77, a longtime partner at the New York City law firm of Fried Frank and the president of the New York County Lawyers Association. For a videotape of the entire program, see Rutgers–Newark, "100 Years, 100 Milestones."

CHAPTER 5

72. *Regents of the University of California v. Bakke*, 438 U.S. 265 (1978).

73. *Brown v. Board of Education*, 347 U.S. 483 (1954).

74. *Doherty v. Rutgers School of Law–Newark*, 651 F.2d 893 (Third Circuit 1981).

75. *Rutgers Law Review* 31, Documents from the Faculty Debates, 857, 858.

76. Ibid., 896.

77. Ibid., 861.

78. Ibid., 857–59.

79. Ibid., 859.

80. Rutgers–Newark, Quick Facts.

81. Rutgers–Newark, Minutes of Faculty Meeting, 3.

82. Rutgers–Newark, Report of the MSP Study Committee.

83. Ibid., 13.

84. Ibid.

85. The meeting had been scheduled for November 9 but was delayed because of Eric Neisser's sudden death.

86. Rutgers–Newark, Minutes of Faculty Meeting. The rest of the description of the meeting is drawn from those minutes.

87. *Grutter v. Bollinger*, 539 U.S. 306 (2003).

88. *Gratz v. Bollinger*, 539 U.S. 244 (2003).

89. *Parents Involved in Community Schools v. Seattle School District No. 1*, 551 U.S. 701 (2007).

90. *U.S. News & World Report*, campus diversity at Rutgers, http://www.usnews.com.

91. 100 N.J. 269 (N.J. 1985). This is the first of twenty New Jersey Supreme Court opinions and orders in *Abbott*, the most recent issued on May 28, 2009.

92. 69 N.J. 449 (N.J. 1976). This is the first of eight opinions and orders in *Robinson*, the last issued on June 15, 1976.

93. Fuetsch, "NJ, the Education State."

94. *Abbott v. Burke* 199, N.J. 140 (N.J. 2009).

95. *Southern Burlington County NAACP v. Mount Laurel Township*, 67 N.J. 151 (1975). This is the first in a complex set of cases dealing with the right to affordable housing, which came to be referred to as the "Mount Laurel Doctrine."

96. See Askin, ed., *"You Can Tell It to the Judge."* Fifteen Rutgers Law faculty members tell their tales about students making law through clinical and other programs. For a broader, more historical perspective, see Wizner, "Law School Clinic," 1929.

97. Rutgers–Newark, *Rutgers Law School News*.

98. *Jama v. Esmor Correctional Services, Inc.*, 577 F.3d 169 (Third Circuit 2009).

99. Rutgers–Newark, Course Catalog, 2007–2009.

100. Students continue to urge the law school to offer other courses relevant to the public interest. For example, they have petitioned for a course regarding legal issues in human reproduction, which would investigate reproductive health and legal regulation of reproduction and the effects on the quality of the United States' civic life and economy, as well as on international development, religion, politics and the status of women.

101. Rutgers–Newark, Minority Student Program (MSP) brochure, 6.

102. Wellen, "$8.78 Million Maneuver," *New York Times*.

103. U.S. General Accountability Office, *Higher Education*.

104. See the weblog for Society of American Law Teachers & Lawyering in the Digital Age Clinic, A Disturbing Trend in Law School Diversity.

105. Frank, "Why Not a Clinical Lawyering School?"

106. This report was issued on behalf of the ABA's Section of Legal Education and Admissions to the Bar. Robert MacCrate, formerly partner and vice-chairman of Sullivan & Cromwell, chaired the task force that produced the report.

107. The authors were Judith Welch Wegner, professor of law and former dean of the University of North Carolina–Chapel Hill; Lee Shulman, president of the Carnegie Foundation for the Advancement of Teaching; and William Sullivan, Lloyd Bond and Anne Colby, senior scholars and program co-director, respectively, at the Carnegie Foundation.

108. Thomson, *Law School 2.0*.

109. This snapshot is drawn from Rutgers–Newark, Quick Facts.

Chapter 6

110. Currier, "Meaning of the Gifts to Education."

111. Kingdon, *John Cotton Dana*.

112. Wechsler, "Brewing Bachelors," 39.

113. Ibid., 40.

114. Ibid.; also quoting from *New York Times*, "Hague Hailed," 23 and *New York Times*, "Finds Hague Fight," 13.

115. Wechsler, "Brewing Bachelors," 39.

116. *Hague v. CIO*, 307 U.S. 496 (1939).

117. Francione and Thomas, "The Wind Was at Our Backs," 472.

118. Axelrod, "Lehan K. Tunks—A Tribute," 569.

119. Ibid.

120. Ibid.

121. Ibid., 570.

122. Ibid.

123. Braun, "Newark Heroine."

124. Francione and Thomas, "The Wind Was at Our Backs," 478.

125. The proceedings of the symposium were published as Haber and Cohen, eds., *Law School of Tomorrow*.

126. Emerson and Haber, *Political and Civil Rights*.

127. Francione and Thomas, "The Wind Was at Our Backs," 484. Unfortunately, Alan Schwarz's last name is consistently misspelled in the article; the error has been corrected in this quotation.

128. Ibid.

129. Ibid.

130. That designation probably had more resonance then. It was an era during which one of the popular jokes involved two friends meeting on the street. One asked, "What do you think about the Indianapolis 500?" The other replied, "They're all innocent and should be freed immediately."

131. Francione and Thomas, "The Wind Was at Our Backs," 477.

132. Goldsmith, "Class of '77 Dedicates Law School Garden."

133. Braun, "A Century's Eccentricity."

134. Braun, "Head of Congressional Oversight Panel."

135. Ibid.

136. Ibid.

CHAPTER 7

137. Rutgers School of Law–Newark, John J. Farmer Jr., Faculty Profile, 2009.

138. Couch, "The Road to Financial Self Sufficiency," *UVA Lawyer* (Spring 2008).

BIBLIOGRAPHY

BOOKS

Administrative Process Project of Rutgers Law School. *Enforcing Fair Housing Laws: Apartments in White Suburbia*. Newark, NJ: Rutgers Law School, July 1970.

Administrative Process Project of Rutgers Law School and New Jersey Division on Civil Rights. *Enforcing Equality in Housing and Employment through State Civil Rights Laws 1969–1972*. Newark, NJ: Rutgers Law School, July 1972.

Askin, Frank. *Defending Rights: A Life in Law and Politics*. Amherst, NY: Prometheus Books, 1997.

Askin, Frank, ed. *"You Can Tell It to the Judge"…and Other True Tales of Law School Lawyering*. Lake Mary, FL: Vandeplas Publishing, 2009.

Calman, Alvin R. *Upsala College: The Early Years*. New York: Vantage Press, 1983.

Consalus, Charles Edward. "The History of Legal Education in New Jersey." PhD dissertation, Doctor of Education, Teachers College, Columbia University, 1979. On file with Rutgers–Newark Law Library.

Denning, Michael. *The Cultural Front: The Laboring of American Culture in the Twentieth Century*. New York: Verso, 1997.

Emerson, Thomas I., and David Haber. *Political and Civil Rights in the United States*. Buffalo, NY: Dennis & Co., Inc., 1952.

Gitlin, Todd. *The Sixties: Years of Hope, Days of Rage*. New York: Bantam Books, 1987.

Guerrero, Andrea. *Silence at Boalt Hall: The Dismantling of Affirmative Action*. Berkeley: University of California Press, 2002.

Haber, David, and Julius Cohen, eds. *The Law School of Tomorrow: The Projection of an Ideal*. Piscataway, NJ: Rutgers University Press, 1968.

Herman, Max A., ed. *The Detroit and Newark Riots of 1967*. Newark, NJ: Rutgers–Newark Department of Sociology and Anthropology, 2002.

Kingdon, Frank. *John Cotton Dana: A Life*. Boston, MA: Merrymount Press, 1940.

Kinoy, Arthur. *Rights on Trial: The Odyssey of a People's Lawyer*. Cambridge, MA: Harvard University Press, 1983.

Lefcourt, Robert, ed. *Law Against the People: Essays to Demystify Law, Order and the Courts*. New York: Vintage Books, 1971.

Legacy yearbooks, New Jersey Law School, University of Newark Law School, Rutgers School of Law–Newark (as merged), 1908–2009.

Leonard, Walter J. "Bakke: Extending the Dream Deferred." In *Towards a Diversified Legal Profession: An Inquiry into the Law School Admission Test, Grade Inflation, and Current Admissions Policies*. Edited by David M. White. New York: National Conference of Black Lawyers, 1981.

McCormick, Richard P. *The Black Student Protest Movement at Rutgers*. Piscataway, NJ: Rutgers University Press, 1990.

National Advisory Commission on Civil Disorders (Kerner Commission). *Report of the National Advisory Commission on Civil Disorders*. New York: Bantam Books, 1968.

Thomson, David I.E. *Law School 2.0: Legal Education for a Digital Age*. New York: LexisNexis/Matthew Bender, 2008.

U.S. General Accountability Office. *Higher Education: Issues Related to Law School Cost and Access* (GAO 10-20). Washington, D.C.: U.S. General Accountability Office, 2009.

ACADEMIC AND JOURNAL ARTICLES

Askin, Frank. "A Law School Where Students Don't Just Learn the Law; They Help Make the Law." Rutgers School of Thought, Symposium 1999. *Rutgers Law Review* 51 (1999): 855.

Axelrod, Allen. "Lehan K. Tunks—A Tribute." *Washington Law Review* 60 (1984–85): 569.

Christensen, Leah M. "The Power of Skills Training: A Study of Lawyering Skills Grades as the Strongest Predictor of Law School Success (Or in Other Words, It's Time for Legal Education to Get Serious About Skills Training if We Care About How Our Students Learn)." TJSL Legal Studies Research Paper No. 1235531, August 18, 2008. http://ssrn.com/abstract=1235531.

Cohen, Lloyd R. "Comments on the Legal Education Cartel." *Journal of Contemporary Legal Issue* 17 (2008). http://papers.ssrn.com/sol3/papers.cfm?abstract_id=1161259.

Deutsch, Stuart L. Untitled introduction. Rutgers School of Thought, Symposium 1999. *Rutgers Law Review* 51 (1999): unnumbered pages.

Francione, Gary L., and George C. Thomas III. "The Wind Was at Our Backs: The Third Golden Period of Rutgers Law School." Centennial Essay. *Rutgers Law Review* 61 (2009): 471–72.

Frank, Jerome. "Why Not a Clinical Lawyering School?" *University of Pennsylvania Law Review* 81 (1933): 907.

Johnson, Alex M., Jr. "Knots in the Law School Pipeline for Students of Color: The LSAT Is Not the Problem and Affirmative Action Is Not the Answer." University of Virginia Legal Working Paper Series, Paper No. 3 (October 2008). http://law.bepress.com/uvalwps/uva_publiclaw/art103.

Lloyd, Brian. "Arthur Kinoy and the Passing of 1960s Radicalism." *Science and Society* (Winter 2004).

Perez, Ignacio. "Doing Battle With Bakke." *Rutgers Law Record* 8 (1978): 1.

Rothman, Andrew. "Preparing Law School Graduates for Practice: A Blueprint for Professional Education Following the Medical Profession Example." Rutgers School of Thought, Symposium 1999. *Rutgers Law Review* 51 (1999): 875.

Rutgers Law Review 51. Rutgers School of Thought, Symposium 1999 (1999): 777.

Rutgers Law Review 31. "Alfred A. Slocum, Report Concurring with the Majority Report of the Admissions Committee." Rutgers Law School Minority Student Program: Documents from the Faculty Debates (1979): 898.

———. "Arthur Kinoy, The Rutgers MSP: Commitment, Experience, and the Constitution." Rutgers Law School Minority Student Program: Documents from the Faculty Debates (1979): 860.

———. "Jonathan Hyman and Annamay T. Sheppard, Admissions Committee, Majority Report." Rutgers Law School Minority Student Program: Documents from the Faculty Debates (1979): 865.

———. "Norman L. Cantor and Alan Schwarz, Admissions Committee, Minority Report." Rutgers Law School Minority Student Program: Documents from the Faculty Debates (1979): 885.

———. Rutgers Law School Minority Student Program: Documents from the Faculty Debates (1979): 857.

———. "Table of Contents, Constitutional Litigation Clinic Brief." Rutgers Law School Minority Student Program: Documents from the Faculty Debates (1979): 903.

Sheppard, Annamay T. "Bricks, Mortar, Heart." Rutgers School of Thought, Symposium 1999. *Rutgers Law Review* 51 (1999): 971.

Taub, Nadine. "The Rutgers–Newark Women's Rights Litigation Clinic: An Old and a New Story?" Rutgers School of Thought, Symposium 1999. *Rutgers Law Review* 51 (1999): 1023.

Thomas George C., III, "Law's Social Consequences." Rutgers School of Thought, Symposium 1999. *Rutgers Law Review* 51 (1999): 845.

Timoney, Kelly. "Rutgers School of Law–Newark and the Legacy of Elizabeth Blume Silverstein." *Women's Rights Law Reporter* 60 (2009): 635, 642.

Tractenberg, Paul. "Using Law to Advance the Public Interest: Rutgers Law School and Me." Rutgers School of Thought, Symposium 1999. *Rutgers Law Review* 51 (1999): 1001.

Wizner, Stephen. "The Law School Clinic: Legal Education in the Interests of Justice." *Fordham Law Review* 70 (2002): 1929.

Cases and Statutes

Abbott v. Burke, 100 N.J. 269 (1985).

Abbott v. Burke, 199 N.J. 140 (2009).

Brown v. Board of Education, 347 U.S. (1954).

Doherty v. Rutgers School of Law–Newark, 651 F.2d 893 (Third Circuit 1981).

Gratz v. Bollinger, 539 U.S. 244 (2003).

Grutter v. Bollinger, 539 U.S. 306 (2003).

Hague v. CIO, 307 U.S. 496 (1939).

Jama v. Esmor Correctional Services, Inc., 577 F.3d 169 (Third Circuit 2009).

Parents Involved in Community Schools v. Seattle School District No. 1, 551 U.S. 701 (2007).

Regents of the University of California v. Bakke, 438 U.S. 265 (1978).

Robinson v. Cahill, 69 N.J. 449 (1976).

Southern Burlington County NAACP v. Mount Laurel Township, 67 N.J. 151 (1975).

N.J.S.A. 18A:65-1 (Thomson Reuters/West, 2008). Short Title, "Rutgers, the State University Law."

N.J.S.A. 18A:65-3 (Thomson Reuters/West, 2008). "The State University" or "The University" defined and described.

NEWS AND PERIODICALS

Alger, Jonathan R. "The Educational Value of Diversity." *Academe*, January–February 1997, 20. Reprinted with permission from *Academe: Bulletin of the American Association of University Professors*, January–February 1997.

Askin, Frank. "An Affirmative Legacy at Rutgers Law," *Star-Ledger*, January 22, 2006, 4

Braun, Robert. "A Century's Eccentricity at Rutgers Law School Yields Legal Greatness." *Star-Ledger*, November 10, 2008. NJ.com blog. http://blog.nj.com/njv_bob_braun/2008/11/a_centurys_eccentricity_at_rut.html.

———. "Head of Congressional Oversight Panel has New Jersey Roots." *Star-Ledger*, June 21, 2009. NJ.com blog. http://blog.nj.com/njv_bob_braun/2009/06/head_of_congressional_oversigh.html.

———. "Newark Heroine Always Preferred the Color Human." *Star-Ledger*, January 19, 1996.

———. "Success and Influence, with Thanks to Rutgers Law." *Star-Ledger*, June 22, 2009.

Cohen, Deborah. "In 1967, Echoes of Newark in Plainfield." NJ.com blog, 1997. http://blog.nj.com/njv_frank_askin/2007/11/rioting_was_not_limited_to.html.

Couch, Cullen. "The Road to Financial Self Sufficiency." *UVA Lawyer* (Spring 2008). http://www.law.virginia.edu/html/alumni/uvalawyer/spr08/financialselfsuffic.htm.

Currier, Richard D. Letter to the Editor. *New York Times*, September 23, 1916.

———. "Meaning of the Gifts to Education." *New York Times*, December 15, 1901, 7.

Goldsmith, Robert S. "Class of '77 Dedicates Law School Garden in Memory of A.J. Smaldone," *Rutgers Tradition* 25 (Fall 2003). The *Tradition* was the alumni magazine of Rutgers School of Law–Newark.

McKeever, Lauren. "Justice For All." *Rutgers* magazine (November–December 1988), 10. On file with Rutgers–Newark Law Library.

Nash, Margo, and Robert Strauss. "Jersey Footlights: Remembering a Revolution." *New York Times*, April 4, 2004, 14NJ 11. See also "Corrections," *New York Times*, April 18, 2004, 14NJ 2.

New York Times. "C. Willard Heckel, Ex-Law Dean, Dies." April 7, 1988.

———. "Elizabeth Silverstein, New Jersey Lawyer, 98." February 5, 1991, B7. Silverstein was a 1911 New Jersey Law School graduate. See also "Who's Who" section in 1931 *Legacy* yearbook.

———. "Finds Hague Fight 'Battle of Century.'" June 17, 1938.

———. "Hague Hailed as Foe of Reds at Service." November 25, 1937.

Nixon, Ferlanda Fox. "Reflections on a Century-Long Tradition of Teaching Students to Think Like Lawyers," *Connections* newsletter (Winter 2009).

Reeves, Richard. "Hatred and Pity Mix in Views of Whites on Newark Negroes." *New York Times*, July 22, 1967.

Robinson, Janice S. "Unlocking the Doors to Legal Education: Rutgers–Newark Law School's Minority Student Program." *New Jersey Lawyer* (November–December 1992): 16. On file with Rutgers–Newark Law Library.

U.S. News & World Report. Best Graduate Schools: How to Use Our Lists Wisely, March 26, 2008. http://www.usnews.com/articles/education/best-graduate-schools/2008/03/26/how-to-use-our-lists-wisely.html.

————. Best Graduate Schools: Information for School Officials, March 26, 2008. http://www.usnews.com/articles/education/best-graduate-schools/2008/03/26/information-for-school-officials.html#1.

————. Best Graduate Schools: Law School Diversity, March 26, 2008. http://www.usnews.com/articles/education/best-graduate-schools/2008/03/26/law-school-diversity.html.

————. Best Graduate Schools: Law School Ranking Methodology, March 26, 2008. http://www.usnews.com/articles/education/best-graduate-schools/2008/03/26/law-methodology.html.

————. "Which Colleges Have the Most Student Diversity," 2009. http://www.usnews.com/blogs/college-rankings-blog/2009/08/27/which-colleges-have-the-most-student-diversity.html.

Waggoner, Walter H. "Malcolm Talbott, Rutgers Professor." *New York Times*, July 10, 1980.

Wellen, Alex. "The $8.78 Million Maneuver." *New York Times*, July 31, 2005.

RUTGERS UNIVERSITY SOURCES

Diner, Steven J. "A Message from the Provost: Remarks at the Commemoration of the Conklin Hall Takeover." Rutgers–Newark, February 24, 2004. http://www.newark.rutgers.edu/provost/index.php?sId=022404.

Haber, David. "Report and Recommendations: Courses of Study Committee," April 14, 1971. On file with Rutgers–Newark Law Library.

Hanks, Eva H. Interdepartmental Communication to Professor David Haber, Chairman of the Curriculum Committee, Rutgers School of Law–Newark, March 31, 1971. On file with Rutgers–Newark Law Library.

Heckel, Willard, Dean. Letter to Dean Russell Fairbanks (RG N7). Special Collections and University Archives, Rutgers University Libraries.

Jarmel, Eli. Memorandum, Chairman of the Sub-Committee on Clinical Education to Curriculum Committee, Rutgers School of Law–Newark, April 13, 1971. On file with Rutgers–Newark Law Library.

Lewis, Jan Ellen, Professor of History and Associate Dean. "Address to the Faculty at Rutgers, Newark: A Brief History of the Red Scare at Rutgers." Rutgers University, March 25, 2009. On file with author.

Newark Evening News. March 21, 1959 (RG N7 G3). Special Collections and University Archives, Rutgers University Libraries.

Rutgers School of Law–Newark. "An Account of the Situation at the South Jersey Division of the School, Oct. 1958" (RG N7 A2b). Special Collections and University Archives, Rutgers University Libraries.

———. Admission Application, 2009. On file with Rutgers–Newark Law Library.

———. "Analysis of Law School Enrollment, 1946" (RG N7 K1). Special Collections and University Archives, Rutgers University Libraries.

———. Committee on Planning and Development, 1958 (RG N7 A2d). Special Collections and University Archives, Rutgers University Libraries.

———. Course Catalog, 2007–2009. http://catalogs.rutgers.edu/generated/nwk-law_current/index.html.

———. "Distinguished Early Alumni" (RG N7 A1). Special Collections and University Archives, Rutgers University Libraries.

———. Fact Sheets, 2006 and 2008. On file with Rutgers School of Law, Newark, Office of Admissions.

———. Faculty Meetings, May 8, 1970; May 14, 1970; September 23, 1970; October 21, 1970; April 21, 1971; and April 26, 1971. On file with Rutgers–Newark Law Library.

———. Faculty Resolution, adopted November 1999. Admissions policy with Appendix B: "Factors to Be Considered in Admissions." On file with Rutgers–Newark Law Library.

———. Faculty Update (RG N7 A2b). Special Collections and University Archives, Rutgers University Libraries.

———. Graduation Statistics, 1909–1950 (GR N7 A2d). Special Collections and University Archives, Rutgers University Libraries.

———. "John J. Farmer Jr." Faculty Profile, 2009. http://law.newark. rutgers.edu/faculty/faculty-profiles/john-j-farmer-jr.

———. Memo on Night Law School, 1955 (RG N7 A2b). Special Collections and University Archives, Rutgers University Libraries.

———. Mercer Beasley (RG N7 A2d). Special Collections and University Archives, Rutgers University Libraries.

———. "Minority Student Program." Admissions & Financial Aid, 2009. http://law.newark.rutgers.edu/admissions-financial-aid/minority-student-program.

———. Minority Student Program (MSP) brochure, 2009. On file with Rutgers–Newark Law Library.

———. Minutes of Faculty Meeting, November 12, 1998. On file with Rutgers–Newark Law Library.

———. Newark Legal Services Project (RG N7 A2b). Special Collections and University Archives, Rutgers University Libraries.

———. "Newark Riots, 1967," December 7, 2008. http://www.67riots. rutgers.edu/n_index.htm.

———. "100 Years, 100 Milestones." 1908–2008 Centennial Celebration, 2009. http://lawwiki.rutgers.edu/100years/100milestones.

———. "Quick Facts." About the School, 2009. http://law.newark.rutgers. edu/about-school/quick-facts.

———. Records of the New Jersey Law School, 1908–1950 (RG N7). *Topics* 1, no. 1 (1925). Special Collections and University Archives, Rutgers University Libraries.

————. Report of the MSP Study Committee (partial dissent of Professor Blumrosen), October 25, 1999. On file with Rutgers–Newark Law Library.

————. "The Roots of the University." A Century of Reaching Higher: 1908–2008. http://www.newark.rutgers.edu/history/index.php?sId=history.

————. *Rutgers Law School News*, April 2006. http://law-library.rutgers.edu/news/newsletters/April2006News&Events.pdf.

————. *Rutgers Law School Newspaper* 1, no. 2 (December 18, 1970). On file with Rutgers–Newark Law Library.

————. September 1968 Plan (RG N7). Special Collections and University Archives, Rutgers University Libraries.

————. Welfare Rights Project (RG N7 A2b). Special Collections and University Archives, Rutgers University Libraries.

————. World Order Models Project (RG N7 A1). Special Collections and University Archives, Rutgers University Libraries.

Talbott, Malcolm. Press Release, March 3, 1969. On file with author.

Tractenberg, Paul. Centennial Day Notes. Rutgers School of Law–Newark, September 9, 2008, edited version September 15, 2008. On file with author.

Tunks, Lehan K., Dean. Letter, 1955 (RG N7 A2d). Special Collections and University Archives, Rutgers University Libraries.

Wechsler, Harold S. "Brewing Bachelors: The History of the University of Newark," 2005. http://www.newark.rutgers.edu/history/history-wechsler.pdf.

INTERNET AND OTHER SOURCES

Affirmative Action in American Law Schools: A Briefing before the United States Commission on Civil Rights. http://www.usccr.gov/pubs/AALSreport.pdf.

American Bar Association. "Equal Opportunity and Diversity in Legal Education." http://www.abanet.org/media/legaled/home.shtml. Site has links to ABA standard for accreditation through August 2006.

Fuetsch, Michele. "NJ, the Education State." *Record*, December 20, 2009. http://www.edlawcenter.org/ELCPublic/elcnews_091221_NJ_ TheEducationState.htm.

Heriot, Gail. "The ABA's Diversity Agenda." Students for Academic Freedom. http://www.studentsforacademicfreedom.org/news/2631/ the-abas-diversity-agenda and http://www.mindingthecampus.com/ originals/2008/07/by_gail_heriot_the_aba.html.

Morse, Robert. "U.S. News Considers Changing Its Law School Ranking Formula, Part 2 (excerpt)." Consus Group. http://consusrankings.com/2008/07/02/ bvus-news-considers-changing-its-law-school-ranking-formula-part-2.

New Jersey Governor's Select Commission on Civil Disorder. *Report for Action*. Trenton: State of New Jersey, February 1968.

Sedillo Lopez, Antoinette. "ABA Council on Legal Education, Outcome Measures Committee Report." Best Practices for Legal Education. http:// bestpracticeslegaled.albanylawblogs.org/2008/09/06/aba-council-on- legal-education-outcome-measures-committee-report.

Siracusa, Carl. "Rutgers University School of Law: A Brief History." Dedication, S.I. Newhouse Center for Law and Justice, 1979.

Society of American Law Teachers. "Equal Opportunity." A review of ABA standards and *Grutter v. Bollinger*. http://www.saltlaw.org/contents/view/210.

Society of American Law Teachers & Lawyering in the Digital Age Clinic. A Disturbing Trend in Law School Diversity weblog. Columbia University School of Law. http://blogs.law.columbia.edu/salt.

Stake, Jeffrey E. The Law School Ranking Game. http://monoborg.law. indiana.edu/LawRank/index.html.

U.S. Census Bureau. "Newark City, New Jersey." General Demographic Statistics, 2005 and 2009. http//factfinder.census.gov.

INDEX

ABOUT THE AUTHOR

This book is the result of a collaborative effort between Professor Paul Tractenberg and the twelve students in his 2008–9 special Centennial Seminar at Rutgers Law School. The students had the idea of producing a book and submitting draft chapters, instead of traditional seminar papers, for the major part of their accountability. Their submissions became the basis of the book, but Professor Tractenberg substantially edited, reorganized and augmented their work, building both on his long experience at Rutgers Law and his own research.

Paul Tractenberg has been a faculty member at the law school since 1970 and during his long tenure there has played a major role in many of the struggles described in this book, including, prominently, the efforts to achieve and maintain student and faculty diversity and to instill in all students a commitment to using law to achieve social justice.

Professor Tractenberg's special personal focus has been on equalizing educational opportunities for disadvantaged and disabled students, especially those living in New Jersey's poor urban areas. In 1973, he established and was the first director of the Education Law Center (ELC), a public interest center whose mission has been to provide legal representation to students and their parents. Since 1981, ELC has represented more than 300,000 urban students in the landmark case of *Abbott v. Burke*. At the end of 1999, New Jersey judges and lawyers overwhelmingly voted *Abbott* as the most important state court decision of the twentieth century. A *New York Times* editorial referred to it as possibly the most important education case since *Brown v. Board of Education*.

Professor Tractenberg's personal involvement in that equalization effort preceded *Abbott* by eleven years, however, through his involvement in the predecessor case of *Robinson v. Cahill*. During the almost forty years of this litigation effort, Professor Tractenberg has argued before the New Jersey Supreme Court fourteen times.

In 2000, Professor Tractenberg took his commitment to equalizing educational opportunity in a new direction by establishing the Rutgers–Newark Institute on Education Law and Policy, an interdisciplinary research project. Since then, the institute has issued influential reports on many major cutting-edge issues, including educational accountability and state intervention in local school districts; school funding and state and local fiscal policies; school choice; school district consolidation and shared services; school governance and mayoral control; and identifying and replicating excellent schools.

In March 2010, the institute launched a major new venture—the Newark Schools Research Collaborative—in partnership with the Newark Public Schools to bring university research capacity to bear on the district's educational challenges.

Another major institute project also involves a partnership, this one known as LEGAL ONE. With the New Jersey Principals and Supervisors Association and the Monmouth-Ocean Educational Services Commission, the institute is providing legislatively mandated professional development programs to thousands of the state's school leaders in school law, school governance and school ethics. Plans are in the works to offer the program to school leaders in other states and to adapt it for New Jersey's teachers.

Professor Tractenberg is still going strong professionally. In his spare time, he is devoted to his wife of thirty-two years, Neimah, and to his son and daughter-in-law and their four young children. He also is well known for his avid, long-distance bicycling and, around Rutgers Law, for his annual bicycle tour auctioned off at the Public Interest Law Foundation fundraiser.